seamless
(or nearly seamless)
KNITS

Andra Knight-Bowman

Martingale®
& COMPANY

Credits

President & CEO — Tom Wierzbicki

Editorial Director — Mary V. Green

Managing Editor — Tina Cook

Developmental Editor — Karen Costello Soltys

Technical Editor — Ursula Reikes

Copy Editor — Liz McGehee

Design Director — Stan Green

Production Manager — Regina Girard

Illustrator — Robin Strobel

Cover & Text Designer — Shelly Garrison

Photographer — Brent Kane

We would like to thank Pier 1 Imports for props used in this book. Some items seen in the photographs may be available at http://www.pier1.com.

Mission Statement

Dedicated to providing quality products and service to inspire creativity.

Seamless (or Nearly Seamless) Knits
© 2011 by Andra Knight-Bowman

Martingale®
& COMPANY

Martingale & Company®
19021 120th Ave. NE, Suite 102
Bothell, WA 98011-9511 USA
www.martingale-pub.com

Printed in China
16 15 14 13 12   8 7 6 5 4 3

Library of Congress Cataloging-in-Publication Data is available upon request.

ISBN: 978-1-60468-028-7

DEDICATION

To Terry M. Bowman, my husband, my friend, and my hero. Without your love and support, I would be nowhere. I love you!

ACKNOWLEDGMENTS

All of the patterns were named after people who have had a significant influence in my life. Thank you all!

Also, a special thank-you to all of the yarn companies that supplied yarn for the garments in this book: Berroco, Cascade Yarns, Crystal Palace Yarns, Frog Tree Yarns, Knitting Fever, Kollage Yarns, Plymouth Yarn Company, Universal Yarn, and Westminster Fibers.

Contents

Welcome to Seamless
(or Nearly Seamless)
Knits!

When I owned a yarn shop, the number-one complaint I heard from my "sweater" knitters was not wanting to sew the pieces together after they were completed. I agree; it's not my favorite task to do either. Over the past few years, I decided to put together some seamless designs and soon realized that there are many different ways to make sweaters seamless and still make them in a range of sizes to fit all figures.

I've arranged this book in categories by how the sweater is made: First, the basic method starting from the bottom of a sweater and working your way up to the shoulders. Second, starting from the shoulders and working your way down to the waist. And, third (and one of my favorites), working in all different directions, usually side to side but combining the other directions along with it.

I hope that you will enjoy this book as much as I enjoyed creating it and, when you sit down to knit, that you get the fulfillment that I have enjoyed for the past 37 years. Leave the stress of sewing seams aside. After all, knitting is our therapy. Isn't knitting supposed to be relaxing?

~ Andra

Here you'll find information on some of the techniques used in this book. Refer to "Abbreviations" on page 78 to familiarize yourself with new terms or to double-check abbreviations.

GAUGE

Checking your gauge before you begin a project is essential, not only to make sure that the finished garment will fit correctly, but also to make sure you like the way the yarn is knitting up on the size needles you're using. To make a gauge swatch, use the stitch pattern and recommended needles. Cast on 20 to 24 stitches and work until your swatch measures 5". Bind off loosely.

To measure the stitch gauge, place a ruler horizontally on the swatch. Mark the beginning and end of 4" with pins and count the stitches between the pins. To measure the row gauge, place a ruler vertically on the swatch. Mark the beginning and end of 4" with pins and count the rows between the pins.

If you have more stitches than recommended, knit another swatch using a larger needle. If you have fewer stitches than recommended, knit another swatch using a smaller needle.

CAST ONS

I read many years ago that there were almost 60 different ways to cast on for knitting. Let me share with you my favorite ways.

Long-Tail Cast On

Normally I use the long-tail cast on, mainly because it's the way I learned first. Not only does the long-tail cast on have great elasticity for sweater bands, but it also has a nice finished look. To make sure your tail is long enough, start with the tail end, wrap around the needle for the desired number of sts, and then make a slipknot.

1. Make a slipknot on one needle. Wrap the tail around your left thumb and the yarn that's connected to the ball around your index finger. Hold both yarn ends in the palm of your hand with your remaining fingers.

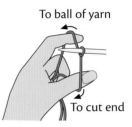

To ball of yarn

To cut end

2. With your right-hand needle, go under the loop on your thumb.

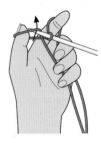

3. Go over the top of the loop on your index finger and bring the yarn through the loop on your thumb. Slip your thumb out of the loop and use it to adjust the tension. You have cast on one stitch.

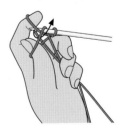

4. Repeat steps 2 and 3 until you have cast on the desired number of stitches.

Cable Cast On

This method is great when making buttonholes and also when casting on at the beginning or end of rows.

1. Make a slipknot and place it on the left-hand needle. Insert the right-hand needle into the stitch, knit it but do not take it off of the left-hand needle. Place the new stitch on the left-hand needle.

2. Insert the right-hand needle between the two stitches on the left-hand needle; knit it as before and place it on the left-hand needle. Continue until you have the desired number of stitches.

Provisional Cast On

There are different ways to create a provisional cast on. This cast on is normally used when you need to remove the original cast-on edge so that you can add on knitting in the opposite direction. For example, when you're knitting a sweater from the top down, by removing the cast on from the shoulders, you won't have any seam at the shoulders. A provisional cast on also looks like the bind-off stitch, so it's good to use when making a sweater from side to side. Use the same yarn as for the body of your garment but don't remove the cast on.

1. Using a crochet hook approximately the same size as your knitting needle and some waste yarn, crochet a loose chain for the desired amount of stitches, adding a few extra chain stitches to be safe. Fasten off and cut the waste yarn.

2. Join the yarn that you're using for your project and pick up the desired amount of stitches through the back loop of the chain.

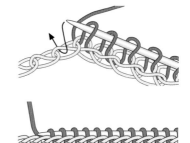

THREE-NEEDLE BIND OFF (3-NEEDLE BO)

The three-needle bind off produces a beautiful finish. It's especially great for shoulder seams.

To work, place stitches to be joined on needles, with the needle points facing to the right and the right sides of your work together. Use a third needle to knit together one stitch from the front needle and one stitch from the back needle. *Knit together the next stitch on the front and back needles. With two stitches on the right-hand needle, bind off by pulling the second stitch over the first stitch and off the needle. Repeat from * until all stitches are bound off.

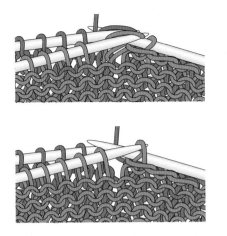

KNITTING IN THE ROUND

Knitting in the round is a common way to eliminate side seams or neck seams. When knitting in the round, make sure that when you join the cast-on stitches into the round they're not twisted around the circular needle. Always place a marker before joining so that you'll know when you've reached the beginning of a new round. Simply place the end of the needle with the last cast-on stitch in your right hand and start knitting or purling to the needle in your left hand.

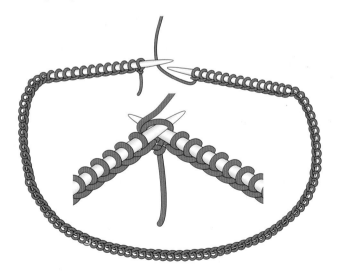

TIPS

- When working in stockinette stitch in the round, knit all stitches in every round.

- When working in garter stitch in the round, purl one round, then knit one round. Continue to alternate the stitches each round until you reach the desired length.

- When reading a charted pattern, each square represents one stitch. When working back and forth, read the chart from right to left on the right side of the work, and from left to right on the wrong side of the work.

- When reading a charted pattern for knitting in the round, read all rounds from right to left.

- When joining a new ball of yarn when you're working in the round, try to join at an inconspicuous area, such as at a side area on the body and underneath a sleeve. If working in a pattern stitch, I've found that joining between a knit and a purl stitch looks the best.

- When weaving in ends, I've found that weaving each tail on the diagonal looks better than weaving them horizontally or vertically.

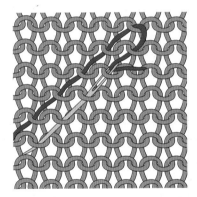

BUILDING FROM THE BOTTOM UP

The patterns in this section are written starting from the bottom hem and working up toward the shoulders. The sleeves are either worked in the same fashion and completed with a join or picked up at the armholes and worked down. Keep in mind, if you want your sweater to be longer than the pattern specifies, the added length should be in the body of the sweater, not after the armhole shaping.

Billie

This sweater proves that an interesting cable doesn't have to be difficult.

Skill Level: Intermediate ◼◼◼◻

Sizes: S (M, L, XL, 2X)

Finished Bust: 36 (40, 44, 48, 52)"

Finished Length: 20½ (21½, 22½, 23½, 24½)"

MATERIALS

4 (4, 5, 5, 6) skeins of King Tut from Knitting Fever (100% finest cotton; 100 g/3.5 oz; 182 yds/166 m) in color 6250 fuchsia ◼4◼

Size 6 (4 mm) circular needles (16" and 32" long)

Size 7 (4.5 mm) circular needle (32" long)

Cable needle

3 stitch markers, 1 in different color for beg of rnd

4 stitch holders

Tapestry needle

Gauge: 20 sts and 25 rows = 4" in St st with smaller needle

DIAMOND CABLE

See chart on page 15 or follow written instructions below.

(Worked over 20 sts)

1/2CBP: Sl 1 st to cn and hold in back, K2, P1 from cn.

2/1CFP: Sl 2 sts to cn and hold in front, P1, K2 from cn.

2/2CF: Sl 2 sts to cn and hold in front, K2, K2 from cn.

Rnds 1, 2, and 4: P8, K4, P8.

Rnd 3: P8, 2/2CF, P8.

Rnd 5: P7, 1/2CBP, 2/1CFP, P7.

Rnd 6: P7, K2, P2, K2, P7.

Rnd 7: P6, 1/2CBP, P2, 2/1CFP, P6.

Rnd 8: P6, K2, P4, K2, P6.

Rnd 9: P5, 1/2CBP, P4, 2/1CFP, K5.

Rnds 10–12: P5, K2, P6, K2, P5.

Rnd 13: P5, 2/1CFP, P4, 1/2CBP, P5.

Rnd 14: Rep rnd 8.

Rnd 15: P6, 2/1CFP, P2, 1/2CBP, P6.

Rnd 16: Rep rnd 6.

Rnd 17: P7, 2/1CFP, 1/2CBP, P7.

Rnd 18: Rep rnd 1.

Rnd 19: Rep rnd 3.

Rnd 20: Rep rnd 1.

Rep rnds 1–20 for patt.

BODY

Body is worked in the rnd up to armholes.

With larger needle, CO 182 (198, 222, 238, 262) sts, pm, join in the rnd.

Setup rnd: K0 (0, 2, 2, 0), *P2, K2*; rep from * to * 9 (10, 11, 12, 14) times, pm, work row 1 of Diamond Cable over next 20 sts, pm, **K2, P2**; rep from ** to ** to last 2 (2, 0, 0, 2) sts, K2 (2, 0, 0, 2).

Work in established patt until body measures 12½ (13, 13½, 14, 14½)".

Change to smaller 32"-long needle, knit 1 rnd, purl 2 rnds.

Divide for front and back: At beg of next rnd, BO 8 (8, 10, 10, 12) sts, K76 (84, 92, 100, 108), BO next 15 (15, 19, 19, 23) sts, K76 (84, 92, 100, 108), BO 7 (7, 9, 9, 11) sts. Fasten off. Put front sts on holder.

BACK

With RS facing, attach yarn and, using smaller 32"-long needle, work back and forth in St st as follows to shape armholes:

Next row: K1, ssk, knit to last 3 sts, K2tog, K1. Turn.

Next row: Purl 1 row even.

Rep last 2 rows 9 (11, 12, 12, 15) more times—56 (60, 66, 74, 76) sts.

Work even in St st until armhole measures 7½ (8, 8½, 9, 9½)", ending with completed WS row.

Place first 13 (14, 15, 17, 17) sts for shoulder on holder, place center 30 (32, 36, 40, 42) sts for back neck on holder, place 13 (14, 15, 17, 17) sts for shoulder on holder.

FRONT

Put front sts from holder on needle. Work as for back to shape armholes and AT THE SAME TIME, when armhole measures 5 (5½, 6, 6½, 7)", ending with completed WS row, shape neck as follows: K18 (19, 20, 22, 22), place center 20 (22, 26, 30, 32) sts on holder, attach new yarn, K18 (19, 20, 22, 22). Turn. Working each side separately, dec 1 st at each neck edge (either K2tog or P2tog) every row 5 times—13 (14, 15, 17, 17) sts for each shoulder.

Work even until armhole measures 7½ (8, 8½, 9, 9½)", ending with completed WS row.

FINISHING

Sew shoulders: Place shoulder sts back on needle. With RS facing tog, join front and back shoulders using 3-needle BO (see page 8).

Neck: With RS facing you, attach yarn and, using smaller 16"-long needle, PU 84 (88, 92, 96, 100) sts, including sts on holders. Work in K2, P2 ribbing for 1½". BO all sts loosely.

Armbands: With RS facing you, attach yarn and, using smaller 16"-long needle, PU 84 (88, 92, 96, 100) sts. Work in K2, P2 ribbing for 1½". BO all sts loosely.

Weave in ends.

Diamond Cable

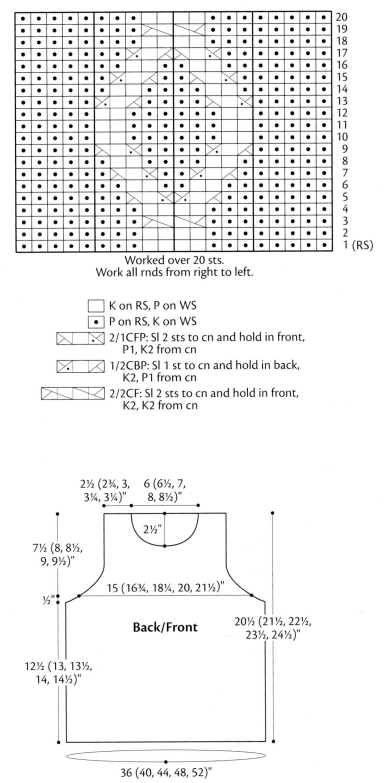

Worked over 20 sts.
Work all rnds from right to left.

☐	K on RS, P on WS
▪	P on RS, K on WS
⟋	2/1CFP: Sl 2 sts to cn and hold in front, P1, K2 from cn
⟍	1/2CBP: Sl 1 st to cn and hold in back, K2, P1 from cn
⟋	2/2CF: Sl 2 sts to cn and hold in front, K2, K2 from cn

2½ (2¾, 3, 3¼, 3¼)" 6 (6½, 7, 8, 8½)"

2½"

7½ (8, 8½, 9, 9½)"

15 (16¾, 18¼, 20, 21½)"

½"

Back/Front

20½ (21½, 22½, 23½, 24½)"

12½ (13, 13½, 14, 14½)"

36 (40, 44, 48, 52)"

This light and airy sweater looks much more challenging than it is. The stitch pattern is easy to follow, and with just one small seam to sew at the neck, finishing is a breeze.

Robin

Sizes: S (M, L, XL, 2X)

Finished Bust: 36 (40, 44, 48, 52)"

Finished Length: 21 (24, 25, 26, 26)"

MATERIALS

8 (9, 10, 11, 12) skeins of Corntastic from Kollage (100% corn; 50 g/1.75 oz; 95 m/105 yds) in color Turquoise 🧶3

Size 4 (3.5 mm) circular needles (16" and 32" long)

Size 6 (4 mm) circular needles (16" and 32" long)

1 stitch marker

3 stitch holders

Tapestry needle

Gauge: 20 sts and 25 rows = 4" in St st with larger needles

PATTERN STITCHES

See charts on page 18 or follow written instructions below.

Pattern 1

(Worked in the rnd over multiple of 10 sts)

Rnds 1 and 2: Purl.

Rnds 3 and 4: Knit.

Rnds 5 and 6: Purl.

Rnd 7: *K4, P3, K3; rep from * around.

Rnd 8: *K3, P3, K4; rep from * around.

Rnd 9: *K2, P3, K5; rep from * around.

Rnd 10: *K1, P3, K6; rep from * around.

Rnd 11: *P3, K7; rep from * around.

Rnd 12: *P2, K7, P1; rep from * around.

Rnd 13: *P1, K7, P2; rep from * around.

Rnd 14: *K7, P3; rep from * around.

Rnd 15: *K6, P3, K1; rep from * around.

Rnd 16: *K5, P3, K2; rep from * around.

Rnd 17: Rep rnd 7.

Rnd 18: Rep rnd 8.

Rnd 19: Rep rnd 9.

Rnd 20: Rep rnd 10.

Rep rnds 1–20 for patt.

Pattern 2

(Worked back and forth over multiple of 5 sts)

Row 1: Knit.

Row 2: *P2, K1, P2; rep from *.

Rep rows 1 and 2 for patt.

BODY

Body is worked in the rnd up to armholes.

Using smaller 32"-long needle, CO 180 (200, 220, 240, 260) sts, pm, join in the rnd. Work K1, P1 ribbing for 8 rnds.

Change to larger 32"-long needle and knit 2 rnds.

Beg patt 1 and rep rnds 1–20 a total of 4 (5, 5, 5, 5) times.

Purl 2 rnds.

Knit 2 rnds.

Purl 2 rnds.

Divide for front and back: K90 (100, 110, 120, 130), place rem sts on holder for front. Turn.

BACK

Beg with row 2, work patt 2 until armhole measures 7 (8, 9, 10, 10)", ending with completed WS row.

Place first 30 (33, 36, 40, 43) sts for shoulder on holder, place center 30 (34, 38, 40, 44) sts for back neck on holder, place 30 (33, 36, 40, 43) sts for shoulder on holder.

FRONT

Place front sts from holder on needle. With RS facing you, attach yarn and work patt 2 for 4 rows.

Shape neck: On next RS row, work 44 (49, 54, 59, 64) sts in established patt, attach new ball of yarn, BO next 2 sts, work to end. Working each side separately, work neck shaping as follows:

> Row 1 (WS): Work in patt.
>
> Row 2 (RS): Work in patt to 3 sts before center, K2tog, K1, switch to 2nd ball of yarn and K1, ssk, work to end.
>
> Rep rows 1 and 2 until 30 (33, 36, 40, 43) sts rem on each side.

Cont in patt until armhole measures 7 (8, 9, 10, 10)", ending with completed WS row.

Sew shoulders: Place shoulder sts back on needle. With RS facing tog, join front and back shoulders using 3-needle BO (see page 8).

SLEEVES

With RS facing you, larger 16"-long needle, and beg at lower armhole, PU 70 (80, 90, 100, 100) sts. Pm, join in the rnd.

Beg patt 1 and rep rnds 1–20 twice.

Purl 2 rnds.

Knit 2 rnds.

Purl 2 rnds.

Change to smaller 16"-long needle, work in K1, P1 ribbing for 7 rnds.

Loosely BO all sts in patt.

FINISHING

Neckband: With RS facing you, smaller 16"-long needle, and beg at bottom right side of neck, PU 114 (128, 142, 156, 162) sts, including back sts on holder. Do not join in the rnd. Work back and forth in K1, P1 ribbing for 7 rows. Loosely BO all sts in patt. Overlapping left front over right front, sew ends of band in place using mattress st on front edge and whipstitch on back edge.

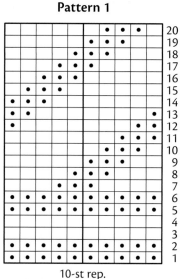

Pattern 1

10-st rep.
Work all rnds from right to left.

Pattern 2

(WS) 2 [·] 1 (RS)

5-st rep

☐ K on RS, P on WS
⊡ P on RS, K on WS

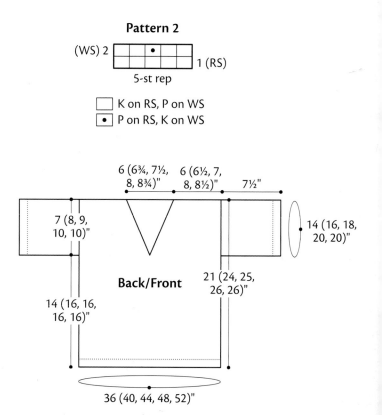

6 (6¾, 7½, 8, 8¾)"   6 (6½, 7, 8, 8½)"   7½"

7 (8, 9, 10, 10)"   14 (16, 18, 20, 20)"

21 (24, 25, 26, 26)"

Back/Front

14 (16, 16, 16, 16)"

36 (40, 44, 48, 52)"

This dress is simple and sexy! By using a yarn that contains some elastic, you won't have a "seat" after sitting.

Angie

Sizes: S (M, L, XL, 2X)

Finished Bust: 36 (40, 44, 48, 52)"

Finished Length: 44 (45, 46, 47, 48)"

MATERIALS

18 (20, 22, 24, 26) skeins of Bamboozle from Crystal Palace Yarns (55% bamboo, 24% cotton, 21% elastic nylon; 50 g/1.75 oz; 83 m/90 yds) in color 9628 Periwinkle

Size 7 (4.5 mm) circular needle (16" long)

Size 8 (4 mm) circular needle (32" long)

4 stitch markers, 1 in different color for beg of rnd

4 stitch holders

Tapestry needle

Gauge: 20 sts and 25 rows = 4" in St st with larger needle

BOTTOM BORDERS (MAKE 2.)

To create a nice edge, start beg of every row with sl1p wyif, return yarn to back, work to end.

With larger needle, CO 90 (100, 110, 120, 130) sts. Sl1p, knit to end. Rep last row 9 more times.

Next row (WS): Sl1p, K5, pm, purl to last 6 sts, pm, K6.

Next row (RS): Sl1p, knit to end.

Rep last 2 rows until piece measures 10" from CO edge. Remove markers at this point. Place sts on holder. Make 2nd border, DO NOT put sts on holder, pm, knit sts from holder, pm, join in the rnd—180 (200, 220, 240, 260) sts.

BODY

Work in St st until piece measures 36½ (37, 37½, 38, 38½)" from CO edge.

BACK

Shape armholes: Sl1p, knit to next marker, turn.

> **Next row (WS):** Sl1p, K5, pm, purl to last 6 sts, pm, K6.
>
> **Next row (RS):** Sl1p, K5, ssk, knit to 2 sts before next marker, K2tog, knit to end.

Rep last 2 rows 12 (13, 14, 15, 16) more times—64 (72, 80, 88, 96) sts.

Work even until armhole measures 7½ (8, 8½, 9, 9½,)", ending with completed WS row.

Place first 17 (19, 21, 22, 24) sts for shoulder on holder, place center 30 (34, 38, 44, 48) sts for back neck on holder, place 17 (19, 21, 22, 24) sts for shoulder on holder.

FRONT

Put sts from holder on needle. With RS facing you, attach yarn and work armhole shaping as for back. AT THE SAME TIME, when armhole measures 5½ (6, 6½, 7, 7½)", ending with completed WS row, shape neck as follows: K22 (24, 26, 27, 29), place center 20 (24, 28, 34, 38) sts on holder, attach yarn, K22 (24, 26, 27. 29). Working each side separately, dec 1 st at each neck edge every row 5 times—17 (19, 21, 22, 24) sts for each shoulder.

Work even until armhole measures 7½ (8, 8½, 9, 9½)", ending with completed WS row.

FINISHING

Sew shoulders: Place shoulder sts back on needles. With RS facing tog, join front and back shoulders using 3-needle BO (see page 8).

Collar: With RS facing, attach yarn at left shoulder and, using smaller 16"-long needle, PU 77 (84, 91, 98, 105) sts, including sts from holders, pm, join in the rnd.

Work in garter st (purl 1 rnd, knit 1 rnd) for 2", then work incs as follows:

Inc rnd: *K7, M1; rep from * around—88 (96, 104, 112, 120) sts.

Work in garter st for 1".

Inc rnd: *K8, M1; rep from * around—99 (108, 117, 126, 135) sts.

Work in garter st for 1".

Inc rnd: *K9, M1; rep from * around—110 (120, 130, 140, 150) sts.

Work in garter st for 1".

BO all sts loosely.

Weave in ends.

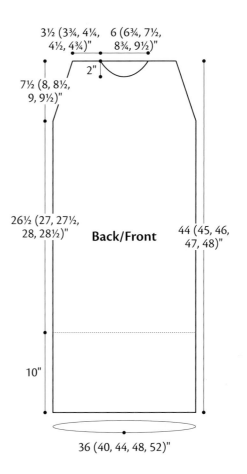

3½ (3¾, 4¼, 4½, 4¾)"   6 (6¾, 7½, 8¾, 9½)"

2"

7½ (8, 8½, 9, 9½)"

26½ (27, 27½, 28, 28½)"

Back/Front

44 (45, 46, 47, 48)"

10"

36 (40, 44, 48, 52)"

Shorter Option

If you're not ready to tackle a long dress, make a short summer top. Follow the instructions for the long dress, but work the bottom borders for 3" and the body until piece measures 12½ (13, 13½, 14, 14½)" from CO edge.

Brooke

Dress it up or down, this "peek-a-boo" sweater is great for any occasion!

Skill Level: Easy ◼◼◻◻

Sizes: S (M, L, XL, 2X)

Finished Bust: 36 (40, 44, 48, 52)"

Finished Length: 21 (22, 23, 24, 25)"

MATERIALS

6 (7, 8, 9, 10) skeins of Fantasy Naturale from Plymouth Yarn (100% mercerized cotton; 100 g/3.5 oz; 95m/140 yds) in color 1404 bright yellow ⓸

Size 7 (4.5 mm) circular needles (16" and 32" long)

Size 9 (5.5 mm) circular needles (16" and 32" long)

8 stitch holders

2 stitch markers in different colors

Cable needle

Tapestry needle

Gauge: 16 sts and 22 rows = 4" in St st with larger needles

BODY

Body is worked in the rnd up to armholes.

With smaller 32"-long needle, CO 144 (160, 176, 192, 208) sts, pm, join in the rnd. Work 3 rows in garter st (knit every rnd). Change to larger 32"-long needle, work in St st until piece measures 13 (13½, 14, 14½, 15)".

Divide for front and back: Work in St st over 72 (80, 88, 96, 104) sts, turn. Place rem sts on needle for front.

BACK

Work in St st until armhole measures 8 (8½, 9, 9½, 10)", ending with completed WS row.

Place first 23 (25, 28, 31, 33) sts for shoulder on holder, place center 26 (30, 32, 34, 38) sts for back neck on holder, place rem 23 (25, 28, 31, 33) sts for shoulder on holder.

FRONT

Place sts from holder on needle. With RS facing you, attach yarn, and work in St st for ½ (1, 1½, 2, 2½)", ending with completed WS row.

Shape neck: K35 (39, 43, 47, 51), place center 2 sts on holder, attach new yarn, K35 (39, 43, 47, 51). Working each side separately, cont until armhole measures 5½ (6, 6½, 7, 7½)", ending with completed WS row. On next RS row, K28 (30, 33, 36, 38), place next 7 (9, 11, 11, 13) sts on holder. On next WS row, P28 (30, 33, 36, 38), place next 7 (9, 11, 11, 13) sts on holder.

Cont in St st, dec 1 st at each side of neck edge every row 5 times—23 (25, 28, 31, 33) sts each side.

Work even until armhole measures 8 (8½, 9, 9½, 10)", ending with completed WS row.

Sew shoulders: Place shoulder sts back on needles. With RS facing tog, join front and back shoulders using 3-needle BO (see page 8).

NECK FINISHING

Keyhole band: With RS facing you, using smaller 16"-long needle, attach yarn at top of left-front separation, PU 36 sts around opening, including 2 center sts from holder. Work 3 rows of garter st. BO all sts loosely.

Neckband: With RS facing you, using smaller 16"-long needle, attach yarn at left shoulder seam, PU 76 (84, 90, 96, 100) sts including sts from holders, pm, join in the rnd. Work 3 rows of garter st. BO all sts loosely.

SLEEVES

With RS facing you, using larger 16"-long needle, attach yarn at shoulder seam, PU 33 (35, 37, 39, 41) sts to underarm, place first marker, PU 33 (35, 37, 39, 41) sts to shoulder—66 (70, 74, 78, 82) sts. Place 2nd marker for beg of rnd, join in the rnd, and knit 1 rnd. Turn and work back and forth as follows:

Row 1 and all odd-numbered rows (WS): K2, purl to last 2 sts before first marker, K2, turn.

Rows 2, 4, 8, 10, 14, 16: Knit to end of row, turn.

Rows 6 and 12: Knit to 2 sts before first marker, K2tog, sl marker, K2tog, knit to end, turn.

Row 18: Sl last 2 sts worked to cn and hold in front, sl 2 sts from RH needle onto LH needle, place sts from cn onto RH needle. The first and last 2 sts have been twisted to join the sleeve. Adjust marker to go between these 4 sts that were just twisted. Knit to 2 sts before first marker K2tog, sl marker, K2tog, knit to end. *This row is worked in the rnd to twist sts. Resume back and forth knitting on row 1.*

Rep rows 1–18 three more times—42 (46, 50, 54, 58) sts.

Change to smaller 16"-long needle. Pm, join in the rnd, and work 3 rnds in garter st.

BO all sts loosely.

Weave in ends.

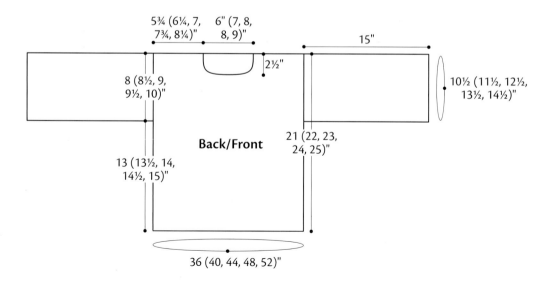

5¾ (6¼, 7, 7¾, 8¼)"

6" (7, 8, 8, 9)"

15"

2½"

10½ (11½, 12½, 13½, 14½)"

8 (8½, 9, 9½, 10)"

Back/Front

21 (22, 23, 24, 25)"

13 (13½, 14, 14½, 15)"

36 (40, 44, 48, 52)"

A very good friend of mine wanted to make a simple garter-stitch vest, so this is what I came up with. It became one of the biggest selling patterns in my shop.

Deb

Skill Level: Easy ◼◼◻◻

Sizes: S (M, L, XL, 2X)

Finished Bust: 38 (42, 46, 50, 54)"

Finished Length: 21 (22, 23, 24, 25)"

MATERIALS

6 (7, 8, 9, 10) skeins of Blackstone Tweed from Berroco (65% wool, 25% superkid mohair, 10% angora rabbit hair; 50 g/1.75 oz; 119 m/130 yds) in color 2623 ◼4◼

Size 7 (4.5 mm) circular needle (32" long)

7 stitch holders

1 button, 2" diameter

Tapestry needle

Gauge: 18 sts and 28 rows = 4" in garter st

BODY

To create a nice edge, start beg of every row with sl1p wyif, return yarn to back, knit to end. Repeat for entire vest.

Right-front border: CO 42 (47, 52, 56, 61) sts. Sl1p, knit to end. Rep this row until piece measures 2½". Place sts on holder.

Back border: CO 84 (94, 104, 112, 122) sts. Work as for right-front border. Place sts on holder.

Left-front border: Work as for right-front border but leave sts on needle, cut yarn.

Join body: Place back sts on same needle, place right-front sts on same needle. With RS facing you, attach yarn at beg and work in established patt until piece measures 13 (14, 14, 14½, 15½)" from CO edge, ending with completed WS row.

RIGHT FRONT

Work over 36 (41, 46, 50, 55) sts, turn, leave rem sts on needle.

Knit 1 row.

Buttonhole: On next RS row, K3, BO 2 sts, knit to last 3 sts, K2tog, K1. On next row, knit to last 3 sts, CO 2 sts (see page 8), K3.

Next row: Knit to last 3 sts, K2tog, K1.

Next row: Sl1p, knit to end.

Rep last 2 rows 3 4 more times—31 (36, 41, 45, 50) sts.

Work even until armhole measures 8 (8, 9, 9½, 9½)", ending with completed WS row. Place first 14 (16, 18, 19, 21) sts for collar on holder, place next 17 (20, 23, 26, 29) sts for shoulder on holder.

BACK

With RS facing you, attach yarn at beg of sts on needle, BO 12 sts, K72 (82, 92, 100, 110), which includes 1 st left over from BO, turn, leave rem sts on needle.

Next row: Knit 1 row.

Next row: Sl1p wyif, ssk, knit to last 3 sts, K2tog , K1.

Rep last 2 rows 4 more times—62 (72, 82, 90, 100) sts.

Work even until armhole measures 8 (8, 9, 9½, 9½)", ending with completed WS row. Place first 17 (20, 23, 26, 29) sts for shoulder on holder, place center 28 (32, 36, 38, 42) sts for collar on holder, place 17 (20, 23, 26, 29) sts for shoulder on holder.

LEFT FRONT

With RS facing, attach yarn at beg of rem sts. BO 12 sts, work to end.

Next row: Knit 1 row.

Next row: Sl1p wyif, ssk, knit to end.

Rep last 2 rows 4 more times—31 (36, 41, 45, 50) sts.

Work even until armhole measures 8 (8, 9, 9½, 9½)", ending with completed WS row. Place first 17 (20, 23, 26, 29) sts for shoulder on holder, place rem 14 (16, 18, 19, 21) sts for front collar on holder.

FINISHING

Sew shoulders: Place shoulder sts back on needles. With RS facing tog, join front and back shoulders using 3-needle BO (see page 8).

Collar: With RS facing you and beg at right-front side, knit sts from holders and PU 3 sts at each shoulder seam. Work in patt for 3". BO all sts loosely.

Sew button opposite buttonhole. Weave in ends.

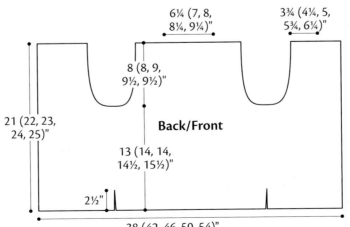

6¼ (7, 8, 8¼, 9¼)"

3¾ (4¼, 5, 5¾, 6¼)"

8 (8, 9, 9½, 9½)"

Back/Front

21 (22, 23, 24, 25)"

13 (14, 14, 14½, 15½)"

2½"

38 (42, 46, 50, 54)"

DEB

Jenny

This is a great vest for us cable junkies.
Because the pattern repeats itself, it's
not too difficult to make.

Skill Level: Intermediate ◼◼◼◻

Sizes: S (M, L, XL, 2X)

Finished Bust: 36 (40, 44, 48, 52)"

Finished Length: 21 (22½, 24, 25½, 26)"

MATERIALS

7 (8, 9, 10, 11) skeins of Jeannee from Plymouth Yarns (51% cotton, 49% acrylic; 50 g/1.75 oz; 101 m/111 yds) in color 6 Sage [4]

Size 6 (4 mm) circular needles (16" and 32" long)

Size 7 (4.5 mm) circular needle (32" long)

8 stitch markers

4 stitch holders

Cable needle

5 buttons, 1" diameter

Tapestry needle

Gauge: 20 sts and 25 rows = 4" in St st with larger needles

PATTERN STITCHES

See charts on page 31 or follow written instructions below.

1/1CB: Sl 1 st to cn and hold in back, K1, K1 from cn.

1/1CBP: Sl 1 st to cn and hold in back, K1, P1 from cn.

1/1CFP: Sl 1 st to cn and hold in front, P1, K1 from cn.

3/3CF: Sl 3 sts to cn and hold in front, K3, K3 from cn.

3/3CB: Sl 3 sts to cn and hold in back, K3, K3 from cn.

Moss Stitch

(Worked over even number of sts)

Rows 1 and 2 (RS): *K1, P1; rep from *.

Rows 3 and 4: *P1, K1; rep from *.

Rep rows 1–4 for patt.

Left Cable

(Worked over 10 sts)

Rows 1, 3, and 7 (RS): P2, K6, P2.

Rows 2, 4, and 6: K2, P6, K2.

Row 5: P2, 3/3CF, P2.

Row 8: K2, P6, K2.

Rep rows 1–8 for patt.

Right Cable

(Worked over 10 sts)

Rows 1, 3, and 7 (RS): P2, K6, P2.

Rows 2, 4, and 6: K2, P6, K2.

Row 5: P2, 3/3CB, P2.

Row 8: K2, P6, K2.

Rep rows 1–8 for patt.

Diamond Cable

(Worked over 16 sts)

Row 1 (RS): P7, 1/1CB, P7.

Row 2: K7, P2, K7.

Row 3: P6, 1/1CBP, 1/1CFP, P6.

Row 4: K6, P1, K2, P1, K6.

Row 5: P5, 1/1CBP, P2, 1/1CFP, P5.

Row 6: K5, P1, K4, P1, K5.

Row 7: P4, 1/1CBP, P4, 1/1CFP, P4.

Row 8: K4, P1, K6, P1, K4.

Row 9: P3, 1/1CBP, P6, 1/1CFP, P3.

Row 10: K3, P1, K8, P1, K3.

Row 11: P2, 1/1CBP, P8, 1/1CFP, P2.

Row 12: K2, P1, K10, P1, K2.

Row 13: P1, 1/1CBP, P2, K6, P2, 1/1CFP, P1.

Row 14: K1, P1, K3, P6, K3, P1, K1.

Row 15: 1/1CBP, P3, K6, P3, 1/1CFP.

Row 16: P1, K4, P6, K4, P1.

Row 17: K1, P4, 3/3CF, P4, P1.

Row 18: P1, K4, P6, K4, P1.

Row 19: 1/1CFP, P3, K6, P3, 1/1CBP.

Row 20: K1, P1, K3, P6, K3, P1, K1.

Row 21: P1, 1/1CFP, P10, 1/1CBP, P1.

Row 22: K2, P1, K10, P1, K2.

Row 23: P2, 1/1CFP, P8, 1/1CBP, P2.

Row 24: K3, P1, K8, P1, K3.

Row 25: P3, 1/1CFP, P6, 1/1CBP, P3.

Row 26: K4, P1, K6, P1, K4.

Row 27: P4, 1/1CFP, P4, 1/1CBP, P4.

Row 28: K5, P1, K4, P1, K5.

Row 29: P5, 1/1CFP, P2, 1/1CBP, P5.

Row 30: K6, P1, K2, P1, K6.

Row 31: P6, 1/1CFP, 1/1CBP, P6.

Row 32: K7, P2, K7.

Rep rows 1–32 for patt.

BODY

Body is worked in one piece up to armholes.

With smaller 32"-long needle, CO 192 (212, 232, 252, 272) sts. Knit 7 rows. Change to larger 32"-long needle and set up patt on next WS row as follows:

S: P6, *K2, P6, K20, P6, K2, P12*; rep from * to * twice, K2, P6, K20, P6, K2, P6.

M: P10, *K2, P6, K20, P6, K2, P16*; rep from * to * twice, K2, P6, K20, P6, K2, P10.

L: P14, *K2, P6, K20, P6, K2, P20*; rep from * to * twice, K2, P6, K20, P6, K2, P14.

XL: P18, *K2, P6, K20, P6, K2, P24*; rep from * to * twice, K2, P6, K20, P6, K2, P18.

2X: P22, *K2, P6, K20, P6, K2, P28*; rep from * to * twice, K2, P6, K20, P6, K2, P22.

Next RS row (all sizes): Work moss st over 6 (10, 14, 18, 22) sts, pm, *work row 1 of left cable over 10 sts, pm, work row 1 of diamond cable over 16 sts, pm, work row 1 of right cable over 10 sts, pm, work moss st over 12 (16, 20, 24, 28) sts, pm*, rep from * to * twice, work row 1 of left cable over 10 sts, pm, work row 1 of diamond cable over 16 sts, pm, work right cable over 10 sts, pm, work moss st over 6 (10, 14, 18, 22) sts.

Cont in established patt until piece measures 13 (14, 15, 16, 16½)" from beg, ending with completed WS row.

Divide for front and back: Work in patt over next 42 (47, 52, 57, 62) sts, BO 12 sts, work in patt over next 84 (94, 104, 114, 124) sts, BO 12 sts, work in patt to end. Turn. Work WS row in patt over next 42 (47, 52, 57, 62) sts, place rem sts on holders.

LEFT FRONT

Next row (RS): K1, ssk, work in patt to last 3 sts, K2tog, K1. Turn.

Next row (WS): P2, work in patt to last 2 sts, P2. Turn.

Rep last 2 rows 5 more times—30 (35, 40, 45, 50) sts.

Working in patt and keeping first 2 sts of armhole in St st, dec 1 st at neck edge only until 20 (23, 26, 30, 33) sts rem.

Work even until armhole measures 8 (8½, 9, 9½, 9½)". Place shoulder sts on holder.

BACK

Place back sts from holder on needle.

Next row (WS): P2, work in patt to last 2 sts, P2. Turn.

Next row (RS): K1, ssk, work in patt to last 3 sts, K2tog, K1.

Rep last 2 rows 5 more times—72 (82, 92, 102, 112) sts.

Work even until armhole measures 8 (8½, 9, 9½, 9½)". Place first 20 (23, 26, 30, 33) sts for shoulder on holder, place center 32 (36, 40, 42, 46) sts for back neck on holder, place 20 (23, 26, 30, 33) sts for shoulder on holder.

RIGHT FRONT

Place front sts from holder on needle.

Next row (WS): P2, work in patt to last 2 sts, P2. Turn.

Next row (RS): K1, ssk, work to last 3 sts, K2tog, K1.

Rep last 2 rows 5 more times—30 (35, 40, 45, 50) sts.

Working in patt and keeping first 2 sts of armhole in St st, dec 1 st at neck edge only until 20 (23, 26, 30, 33) sts rem.

Work even until armhole measures 8 (8½, 9, 9½, 9½)".

FINISHING

Sew shoulders: Place shoulder sts back on needles. With RS facing tog, join front and back shoulders using 3-needle BO (see page 8).

Front band: With RS facing you, smaller 32"-long needle, and beg at right bottom edge, *PU 1 st in next 2 sts, sk next st*, rep from * to * around to sts on holder, knit all sts from holder, rep from * to * to end. Knit 3 rows. Work buttonholes on next RS row as follows:

For S and M only: K3, *YO, K2tog, K12*; rep from * to * 4 times, knit to end.

For L, XL, and 2X only: K3, *YO, K2tog, K11*; rep from * to * 4 times, knit to end.

Knit 3 more rows. BO all sts loosely.

Armbands: With RS facing you and smaller 16"-long needle, PU as for front band, pm, join in the rnd. Work in garter st (knit 1 rnd, purl 1 rnd) for 7 rnds. BO all sts loosely.

Weave in ends.

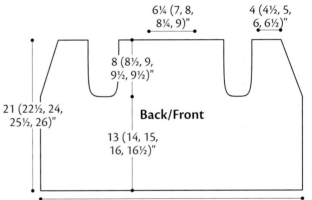

6¼ (7, 8, 8¼, 9)"

4 (4½, 5, 6, 6½)"

8 (8½, 9, 9½, 9½)"

Back/Front

21 (22½, 24, 25½, 26)"

13 (14, 15, 16, 16½)"

36 (40, 44, 48, 52)"

Right Cable

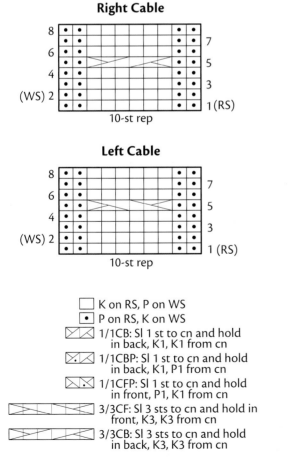

8   7
6   5
4   3
(WS) 2   1(RS)

10-st rep

Left Cable

8   7
6   5
4   3
(WS) 2   1 (RS)

10-st rep

☐ K on RS, P on WS

• P on RS, K on WS

⬚ **1/1CB:** Sl 1 st to cn and hold in back, K1, K1 from cn

⬚ **1/1CBP:** Sl 1 st to cn and hold in back, K1, P1 from cn

⬚ **1/1CFP:** Sl 1 st to cn and hold in front, P1, K1 from cn

⬚ **3/3CF:** Sl 3 sts to cn and hold in front, K3, K3 from cn

⬚ **3/3CB:** Sl 3 sts to cn and hold in back, K3, K3 from cn

Diamond Cable

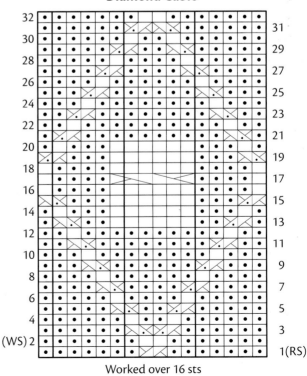

32   31
30   29
28   27
26   25
24   23
22   21
20   19
18   17
16   15
14   13
12   11
10   9
8   7
6   5
4   3
(WS) 2   1(RS)

Worked over 16 sts

JENNY

Dixie

For this easy, classic sweater I used a solid-colored yarn for the body and sleeves, and a hand-dyed yarn that has a mottled effect for the ribbing. But it would look just as good in an all-solid color. If you don't want a high collar, you can simply knit fewer rows to make yours shorter.

Skill Level: Easy ◼◼◻◻

Sizes: S (M, L, XL, 2X)

Finished Bust: 36 (40, 44, 48, 52)"

Finished Length: 22 (23, 24, 25, 26)"

MATERIALS

MC 6 (7, 8, 9, 10) skeins of Cloud 9 from Cascade Yarns (50% merino wood, 50% angora; 50 g/1.75 oz; 99 m/109 yds) in color 104 red ◖4◗

CC 2 (3, 3, 4, 4) skeins of Jewel Hand Dyed from Cascade Yarns (100% Peruvian highland wool; 100 g/3.5 oz; 130 m/142 yds) in color 9969 red ◖4◗

Size 7 (4.5 mm) circular needles (16" and 32" long)

Size 9 (5.5 mm) circular needles (16" and 32" long)

1 stitch marker

4 stitch holders

Tapestry needle

Gauge: 16 sts and 22 rows = 4" in St st with MC and larger needle

BODY

Body is worked in the rnd up to armholes.

With CC and smaller 32"-long needle, CO 144 (160, 176, 192, 208) sts, pm, join in the rnd. Work in K2, P2 ribbing for 4".

Change to MC and larger 32"-long needle. Work in St st until piece measures 14 (14½, 15, 15½, 16)" from beg, ending with completed WS row.

Divide for front and back: On next RS row, work in St st over 72 (80, 88, 96, 104) sts, turn. Place rem sts on holder.

BACK

Work back sts in St st until armhole measures 8 (8½, 9, 9½, 10)", ending with completed WS row. Place 18 (20, 22, 24, 26) sts for shoulder on holder, place center 36 (40, 44, 48, 52) sts for back neck on holder, place 18 (20, 22, 24, 26) sts for shoulder on holder.

FRONT

Place front sts from holder on needle. With RS facing you, attach MC. Knit 1 row. Purl 1 row.

Shape neck: K35 (39, 43, 47, 51) sts, attach 2nd ball of yarn, BO center 2 sts, knit to end. Work both sides separately.

Next row (WS): Purl 1 row.

Next row (RS): Knit to 3 sts before center, K2tog, K1, K1, ssk, work to end.

Rep last 2 rows 16 (18, 20, 22, 24) more times—18 (20, 22, 24, 26) sts each shoulder.

Work even until armhole measures 8 (8½, 9, 9½, 10)", ending with completed WS row.

Sew shoulders: Place shoulder sts back on needles. With RS facing in, join front and back shoulders using 3-needle BO (see page 8).

SLEEVES

With RS facing and larger 16"-long needle, attach MC at underarm seam and PU 64 (68, 72, 76, 80) sts, pm, join in the rnd. Work in St st for 1", ending with completed WS row.

Dec row: K2tog, knit to last 2 sts, K2tog. Cont in St st and work dec every fourth row 11 (13, 13, 15, 15) more times—40 (40, 44, 44, 48) sts.

Work even until sleeve measures 13 (13½, 14, 14, 14)".

Change to CC and smaller 16"-long needle. Work in K2, P2 ribbing for 4". BO all sts in patt loosely.

FINISHING

Collar: With RS facing you, smaller 32"-long needle, and beg at base of right-front neck, attach CC and PU 102 (110, 118, 126, 134) sts. DO NOT join in the rnd. Turn.

> **Next row (WS):** K3 *P2, K2; rep from * to last 3 sts, P3.

> **Next row (RS):** K3, *P2, K2; rep from * to last 3 sts, P3.

Rep last 2 rows until collar measures 4", ending with completed WS row. BO all sts in patt loosely.

Sew collar, overlapping right front over left front. Use mattress st on front edge and whipstitch on back edge.

Weave in ends.

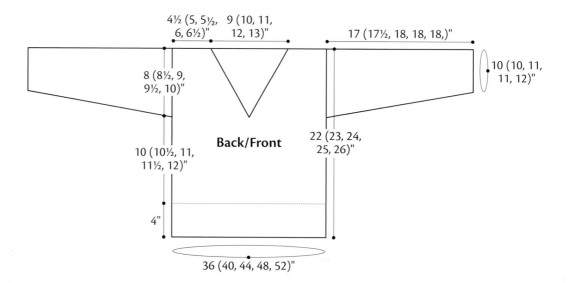

April

Simple garter and stockinette stitches are used in this sweater, making it perfect for a beginner or an advanced knitter who wants an easy, yet stylish project. The asymmetrical design is flattering for all figures. And the only finishing work is a 3" to 4" seam, depending on size, under each arm!

Skill Level: Easy ◼◼◻◻

Sizes: S (M, L, XL, 2X)

Finished Bust: 36 (40, 44, 48, 52)" buttoned

Finished Length: 20 (21½, 22¼, 23¾, 25¼)"

MATERIALS

5 (6, 7, 8, 9) skeins of Felted Tweed from Rowan (50% merino wool, 25% alpaca, 25% viscose; 50 g/1.75 oz; 175 m/191 yds) in color 158 Pine ③

Size 7 (4.5 mm) circular needles (16" and 32" long)

Waste yarn or spare circular needle size 7 or smaller

6 stitch markers

Tapestry needle

1 button, 2" diameter*

*I used a decorative plastic button with a series of holes in it and attached it by making a simple cross-stitch design using the same yarn as the sweater.

Gauge: 20 sts and 25 rows = 4" in St st

Edge Stitches

To create a nice edge, start the beginning of every row with sl1p wyif, then return yarn to back and work to end.

BODY

Body is worked in one piece up to armholes.

With 32"-long needle, CO 190 (210, 230, 250, 270) sts. Do not join in the rnd.

Sl1p, knit to end. Rep this row for 2", ending with completed WS row.

Next row (RS): Sl1p, K9, pm, K50 (55, 60, 65, 70), pm, K90 (100, 110, 120, 130), pm, K30 (35, 40, 45, 50), pm, K10.

Next row (WS): Sl1p, K9, purl to last marker, K10.

Rep last 2 rows until piece measures 11½ (12, 12½, 13, 13½)", ending with completed WS row.

Shape armholes: With RS facing, work to 7 (8, 9, 10, 11) sts before 2nd marker, BO next 14 (16, 18, 20, 22) sts, remove marker, work to 7 (8, 9, 10, 11) sts before 3rd marker, BO next 14 (16, 18, 20, 22) sts, knit to end. Leave sts on needle. Remove 2nd and 3rd markers.

SLEEVES

With 16"-long needle, CO 70 (76, 82, 88, 94) sts, pm, join in the rnd. Work in garter st (purl 1 rnd, knit 1 rnd) for 2". Change to St st and work until sleeve measures 11 (11½, 12, 12½, 13)". At beg of next rnd, BO 7 (8, 9, 10, 11) sts, work to last 7 (8, 9, 10, 11)) sts before marker, and BO to marker—56 (60, 64, 68, 72) sts. Place rem sts on waste yarn or spare needle.

JOIN BODY AND SLEEVES

With WS facing you, work in patt across left front of body to armhole, pm, P56 (60, 64, 68, 72) from WS of sleeve, pm, work in patt across back to armhole, pm, P56 (60, 64, 68, 72) from WS of sleeve, pm, work in patt across right front—274 (298, 322, 346, 370) sts.

SHAPE RAGLAN

Next row (RS): Work 10 sts in patt, sl marker, *work to 2 sts before next marker, K2tog, sl marker, ssk*, rep from * to * 3 more times, work to end.

Next row (WS): Work 1 row even.

Rep last 2 rows 21 (23, 25, 27, 28) more times, ending with completed WS row—98 (106, 114, 122, 138) sts.

NECKBAND

Beg on next RS row, *sl1p, work in garter st to end; rep from * for 1", ending with completed WS row. On next RS row, create buttonhole as follows: Sl1p, K2, BO 3 sts, knit to end, turn. Work 1 row, casting on 3 sts over BO sts (see page 8). Work 1" more in patt. BO all sts loosely.

FINISHING

Sew underarm seams. Sew button opposite buttonhole. Weave in ends.

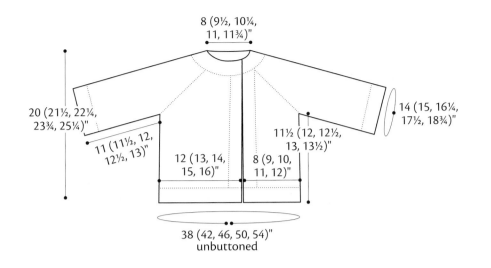

8 (9½, 10¼, 11, 11¾)"

20 (21½, 22¼, 23¾, 25¼)"

14 (15, 16¼, 17½, 18¾)"

11 (11½, 12, 12½, 13)"

11½ (12, 12½, 13, 13½)"

12 (13, 14, 15, 16)"

8 (9, 10, 11, 12)"

38 (42, 46, 50, 54)"
unbuttoned

This clever cardigan/pullover combo features a unique twist closure.
The hood and pockets make it perfect for a cool, brisk stroll.

Kathleen

Skill Level: Intermediate ■■■□

Sizes: S (M, L, XL, 2X)

Finished Bust: 37 (41, 45, 49, 53)"

Finished Length: 23 (24, 25, 26, 27)"

MATERIALS

6 (7, 8, 9, 10) skeins of Deluxe Worsted from Universal Yarn (100% wool; 100 g/3.5 oz; 200 m/220 yds) in color 12256 Orange Splash ④

Size 8 (5 mm) circular needles (16" and 32" long) and double-pointed needles

6 stitch markers

4 stitch holders

Tapestry needle

Gauge: 18 sts and 25 rows = 4" in St st

PATTERN STITCHES

Moss Stitch

(Worked over odd number of sts)

Row 1 (RS): *K1, P1; rep from * to last st, K1.

Row 2: Knit the knit sts and purl the purl sts as they face you.

Row 3: *P1, K1; rep from * to last st, P1.

Row 4: Knit the knit sts and purl the purl sts as they face you.

Rep rows 1–4 for patt.

Stockinette Stitch

(Worked over any number of sts)

Row 1 (RS): Knit.

Row 2: Purl.

Rep rows 1 and 2 for patt.

Reverse Stockinette Stitch

(Worked over any number of sts)

Row 1 (RS): Purl.

Row 2: Knit.

Rep rows 1 and 2 for patt.

Moss Stitch Diamond

See chart on page 41 or follow written instructions below.

(Worked over 21 sts)

Row 1 (RS): P10, K1, P10.

Row 2 and all even-numbered rows: Knit the knit sts and purl the purl sts as they face you.

Row 3: P9, K3, P9.

Row 5: P8, K5, P8.

Row 7: P7, K3, P1, K3, P7.

Row 9: P6, K3, P1, K1, P1, K3, P6.

Row 11: P5, K3, (P1, K1) twice, P1, K3, P5.

Row 13: P4, K3, (P1, K1) 3 times, P1, K3, P4.

Row 15: P3, K3, (P1, K1) 4 times, P1, K3, P3.

Row 17: P2, K3, (P1, K1) 5 times, P1, K3, P2.

Row 19: Rep row 15.

Row 21: Rep row 13.

Row 23: Rep row 11.

Row 25: Rep row 9.

Row 27: Rep row 7.

Row 29: Rep row 5.

Row 31: Rep row 3.

Row 33: Rep row 1.

Row 34: Rep row 2.

Work rows 1–34 once.

POCKET LININGS (MAKE 2.)

CO 21 sts. Work in St st for 34 rows. Place sts on holder and set aside.

BODY

Body is worked in one piece up to armholes.

CO 167 (185, 203, 221, 239) sts. Work in moss st for 9 rows.

Next row (RS): Work in moss st over 7 sts, work 1 st in rev St st, work in St st to last 8 sts, work 1 st in rev St st, work in moss st over rem 7 sts.

Work in patt for 3 more rows.

Next row (RS): Keeping in patt, work 11 (13, 15, 17, 19) sts, pm, work moss st diamond over 21 sts, pm, work 10 (12, 15, 17, 20) sts, pm, work 83 (93, 101, 111, 119) sts, pm, work 10 (12, 15, 17, 20) sts, pm, work moss st diamond over 21 sts, pm, work 11 (13, 15, 17, 19) sts. Work 34 rows of moss st diamond.

Attach pockets: Keeping in patt, work 11 (13, 15, 17, 19) sts, *remove marker, place next 21 sts of moss st diamond on holder, work in St st over 21 sts from one pocket lining, remove next marker,* work to 5th marker, rep from * to *, work in patt to end. You'll now have only 2 markers, one on each side of back sts.

Cont in patt until piece measures 15½ (16, 16½, 17, 17½)", ending with completed RS row, turn.

Work cable twist: With dpns, work back and forth in moss st over next 7 sts for 4 rows. Leave sts on needle. Slide first 7 sts from right front to dpn. With WS facing you, attach yarn and work back and forth in moss st for 4 rows, leave sts on dpn. Holding fronts tog, wrap sts from right-front dpn around sts from left-front dpn once. Place sts back on circular needle. With WS facing you, work 1 row in patt as established.

RIGHT FRONT

Work in patt to first marker, turn. Cont in patt until armhole measures 7½ (8, 8½, 9, 9½)", ending with completed WS row. Place 20 (22, 26, 27, 28) sts for hood on holder, place 22 (24, 25, 28, 32) sts for shoulder on holder.

BACK

With RS facing you, attach yarn and work in St st to next marker for 7½ (8, 8½, 9, 9½)", ending with completed WS row. Place first 22 (24, 25, 28, 32) sts on holder for shoulder, place center 39 (45, 51, 55, 55) sts for hood on holder, place 22 (24, 25, 28, 32) sts for shoulder on holder.

LEFT FRONT

With RS facing you, attach yarn and work in patt for 7½ (8, 8½, 9, 9½)", ending with completed WS row. Place first 22 (24, 25, 28, 32) sts for shoulder on holder, place 20 (22, 26, 27, 28) sts for hood on holder.

Sew shoulders: Place shoulder sts back on needles. With RS facing tog, join front and back shoulders using 3-needle BO (see page 8).

HOOD

Next row (RS): With RS facing you and maintaining patt, work sts from right-front holder, PU 3 sts at shoulder seam, work sts from back holder, PU 3 sts at shoulder seam, work rem sts from left-front holder—85 (95, 109, 115, 117) sts. Turn.

Next row (WS): Work in patt over 42 (47, 54, 57, 58) sts, pm, P1, pm, work to end. Work in patt for 4 rows.

Inc row (RS): Work to marker, M1, sl marker, K1, sl marker, M1, work to end.

Maintaining patt, rep inc row every 6th row 9 times—103 (113, 127, 133, 135) sts.

Work even until hood measures 12" from PU row, ending with completed WS row.

Put half of sts on another needle, bring needles tog, and work 3-needle BO; there will be an extra st on 1 needle; simply knit them tog on last st.

SLEEVES

With RS facing, 16"-long needle, and beg at lower armhole, PU 68 (72, 76, 80, 84) sts, pm, join in the rnd. Work in St st until sleeve measures 15".

Work in moss st for 8 rows.

BO all sts in patt.

FINISHING

Place pocket sts from holder on needle, attach yarn, and work 8 rows in moss st. BO all sts loosely. Rep for other pocket. Sew sides of pocket edge down using mattress st. Whipstitch pocket linings on WS of garment. Weave in ends.

Moss Stitch Diamond

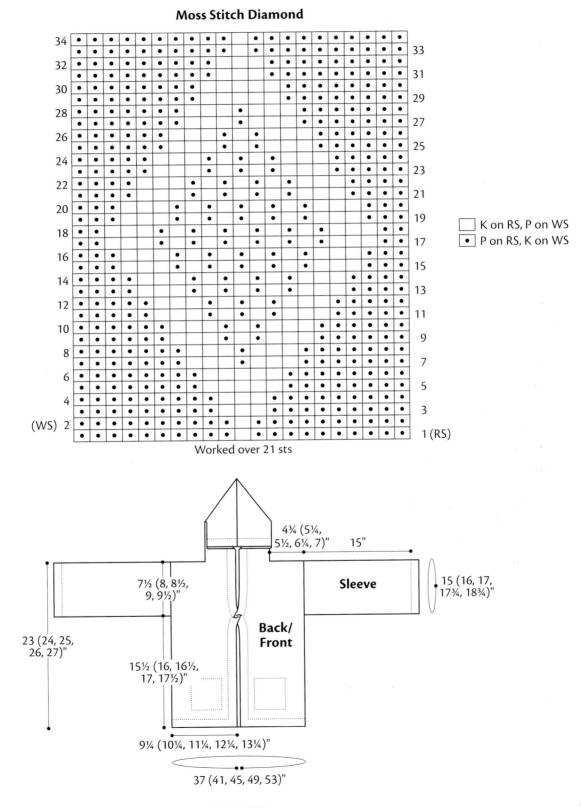

☐ K on RS, P on WS
• P on RS, K on WS

Worked over 21 sts

4¾ (5¼, 5½, 6¼, 7)"   15"

Sleeve

15 (16, 17, 17¾, 18¾)"

7½ (8, 8½, 9, 9½)"

Back/ Front

23 (24, 25, 26, 27)"

15½ (16, 16½, 17, 17½)"

9¼ (10¼, 11¼, 12¼, 13¼)"

37 (41, 45, 49, 53)"

Judy

I got the idea for this fun jacket when my friend Judy showed me a picture of a suede jacket with knitted sleeves.

Skill Level: Easy ◼◼◻◻

Sizes: S (M, L, XL, 2X)

Finished Bust: 38 (42, 46, 50, 54)" buttoned

Finished Length: 23 (24, 25, 26, 27)"

MATERIALS

6 (7, 8, 9, 10) skeins of Ultra Alpaca from Berroco (50% alpaca, 50% wool; 100 g/3.5 oz; 198 m/215 yds) in color 6274 Tiger's Eye (◆4)

Size 5 (3.75 mm) circular needle (32" long)

Size 7 (4.5 mm) circular needles (16" and 32" long)

Waste yarn or spare circular needle size 7 or smaller

4 stitch markers

Tapestry needle

1 button, 2" diameter

Gauge: 20 sts and 26 rows = 4" in St st with larger needle

BODY

Body is worked in one piece up to armholes.

With smaller needle, CO 200 (220, 240, 260, 280) sts. Do not join in the rnd. Knit 3 rows.

Change to larger 32"-long needle and work in St st until piece measures 14 (14½, 15, 15½, 16)", ending with completed RS row.

Shape armhole: On next row (WS), P45 (50, 55, 60, 65), BO 13 sts, P84 (94, 104, 114, 124), BO 13 sts, P45 (50, 55, 60, 65). Leave sts on needle.

SLEEVES

With 16"-long needle, CO 72 (74, 76, 78, 80) sts, pm, join in the round. Work in K1, P1 ribbing for 20½".

BO 7 sts in patt, work in patt to last 6 sts, BO 6 sts in patt—59 (61, 63, 65, 67) sts. Place sts on waste yarn or spare needle.

ATTACH SLEEVES TO BODY AND SHAPE RAGLAN

With RS facing you, K45 (50, 55, 60, 65) from right front, work K1, P1 ribbing over 59 (61, 63, 65, 67) sts from sleeve, pm, K84 (94, 104, 114, 124) from back, pm, work K1, P1 ribbing over 59 (61, 63, 65, 67) sts from other sleeve, pm, K45 (50, 55, 60, 65) from left front in St st—292 (316, 340, 364, 388) sts.

Work 1 row even.

Dec row (RS): Work in patt to 2 sts before first marker, K2tog, sl marker, ssk, rep dec at 2nd, 3rd, and 4th markers, work to end (8-st dec)—284 (308, 332, 356, 380) sts.

Work 1 row even.

Rep dec row EOR 7 more times—228 (252, 276, 300, 324) sts.

Work even until armhole measures 4 (4½, 5, 5½, 6)".

SHAPE YOKE

Entire yoke is worked in garter st.

Work in garter st for 1½", ending with completed WS row.

Dec row (RS): K1, K2tog, *K2, K2tog, rep from * to last st, K1—171 (189, 207, 225, 243) sts.

Work even until yoke measures 3½", ending with completed WS row.

Make buttonhole (RS): K3, BO 3 sts, work to end, turn. Work 1 row, casting on 3 sts over bound-off sts (see "Cable Cast-On" on page 8).

Work even until yoke measures 4", ending with completed WS row.

Dec row (RS): *K1, K2tog; rep from * to end—114 (126, 138, 150, 162) sts.

Work even until yoke measures 5", ending with completed WS row.

Dec row (RS): *K2tog; rep from * to end—57 (63, 69, 75, 81) sts. BO all sts loosely.

FINISHING

Right front edge: With RS facing you and starting at lower edge, *PU 1 st in next 2 sts, skipping 3rd st; rep from * to neck edge. Knit 3 rows. BO all sts loosely.

Left front edge: Work as for right edge except PU sts from neck edge down to lower edge.

Sew underarm seams. Sew button opposite to buttonhole. Weave in ends.

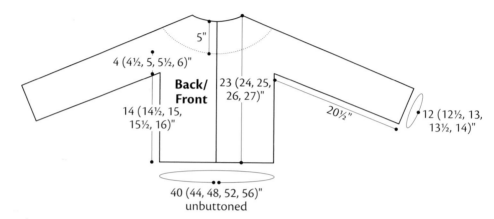

5"

4 (4½, 5, 5½, 6)"

Back/ Front

23 (24, 25, 26, 27)"

14 (14½, 15, 15½, 16)"

20½"

12 (12½, 13, 13½, 14)"

40 (44, 48, 52, 56)"
unbuttoned

JUDY

TAKING IT FROM THE TOP DOWN

All of the sweaters in this section are made by starting at the shoulders and working your way down to the bottom. Knitting in this direction makes it easy to lengthen or shorten a sweater or the sleeves. Don't be intimidated by the provisional cast on.

I used a ribbonlike yarn that allows the sweater to drape just beautifully. Other yarns work well, too, as long as they don't have much texture. This sweater has a deep V-neck, so it could have something worn underneath it.

Sandi

Skill Level: Intermediate ◼◼◼◻

Sizes: S (M, L, XL, 2X)

Finished Bust: 36 (40, 44, 48, 52)"

Finished Length: 21 (22, 23, 24, 25)"

MATERIALS

10 (11, 12, 13, 14) skeins of Bonsai from Berroco (97% bamboo, 3% nylon; (50 g/1.75 oz; 71 m/77 yds) in color 4103 Bamboo ❨4❩

Size 5 (3.75 mm) circular needles (16" and 32" long)

Size 7 (4.5 mm) circular needle (16" and 32" long)

Waste yarn to hold stitches

10 stitch markers

Cable needle

Tapestry needle

Gauge: 20 sts and 25 rows = 4" in St st with larger needle

DOUBLE DIAMOND

See chart on page 49 or follow written instructions below.

(Worked over 22 sts)

1/1CB: Sl 1 st to cn and hold in back, K1, K1 from cn.

1/1CF: Sl 1 st to cn and hold in front, K1, K1 from cn.

1/1CBP: Sl 1 st to cn and hold in back, K1, P1 from cn.

1/1CFP: Sl 1 st to cn and hold in front, P1, K1 from cn.

Rnd 1: K10, 1/1CB, K10.

Rnd 2: K9, 1/1CBP, 1/1CFP, K9.

Rnds 3, 5, 7, 9, 11, 15, 17, 19, 21, 23, 25, 27, 31, 33, 35, 37, 39: Knit the knit sts and purl the purl sts as they face you.

Rnd 4: K8, 1/1CBP, P2, 1/1CFP, K8.

Rnd 6: K7, 1/1CBP, P4, 1/1CFP, K7.

Rnd 8: K6, 1/1CBP, P6, 1/1CFP, K6.

Rnd 10: K5, 1/1CBP, P8, 1/1CFP, K5.

Rnd 12: K4, 1/1CBP, P4, K2, P4, 1/1CFP, K4.

Rnd 13: K5, P5, 1/1CB, P5, K5.

Rnd 14: K3, 1/1CBP, P4, 1/1CB, 1/1CF, P4, 1/1CFP, K3.

Rnd 16: K2, 1/1CBP, P4, 1/1CB, K2, 1/1CF, P4, 1/1CFP, K2.

Rnd 18: K1, 1/1CBP, P4, 1/1CB, K4, 1/1CF, P4, 1/1CFP, K1.

Rnd 20: 1/1CBP, P4, 1/1CB, K6, 1/1CF, P4, 1/1CFP.

Rnd 22: 1/1CF, P4, 1/1CFP, K6, 1/1CBP, P4, 1/1CB.

Rnd 24: K1, 1/1CF, P4, 1/1CFP, K4, 1/1CBP, P4, 1/1CB, K1.

Rnd 26: K2, 1/1CF, P4, 1/1CFP, K2, 1/1CBP, P4, 1/1CB, K2.

Rnd 28: K3, 1/1CF, P4, 1/1CFP, 1/1CBP, P4, 1/1CB, K3.

Rnd 29: K5, P5, 1/1CB, P5, K5.

Rnd 30: K4, 1/1CF, P10, 1/1CB, K4.

Rnd 32: K5, 1/1CF, P8, 1/1CB, K5.

Rnd 34: K6, 1/1CF, P6, 1/1CB, K6.

Rnd 36: K7, 1/1CF, P4, 1/1CB, K7.

Rnd 38: K8, 1/1CF, P2, 1/1CB, K8.

Rnd 40: K9, 1/1CF, 1/1CB, K9.

Rep rnds 1–40 twice.

For neck, inc 1 st after first and before last marker on every fourth row a total of 13 (14, 15, 19, 19) times. AT THE SAME TIME work incs for body and sleeves on EOR a total of 23 (27, 28, 29, 34) times as follows: Inc 1 st before 2nd and after 3rd markers, before 4th and after 5th markers, before 6th and after 7th markers, before 8th and after 9th markers—264 (300, 312, 344, 384) sts. Do not turn. Remove all markers.

JOIN AND WORK BODY

K11, pm, K27 (32, 34, 39, 44), CO 14 (14, 20, 20, 20) sts (see "Cable Cast On" on page 8), sl 56 (65, 66, 72, 82) sleeve sts to waste yarn, K76 (86, 90, 100, 110), CO 14 (14, 20, 20, 20) sts, sl 56 (64, 66, 72, 82) sleeve sts to waste yarn , K27 (32, 34, 39, 44), pm, K11.

Knit 1 rnd.

On next rnd, start double diamond patt at 2nd marker. Cont in patt, working rows 1–40 of chart twice, then cont in St st until piece measures 20½ (21½, 22½, 23½, 24½)" from shoulders.

Change to smaller 32"-long needle. Purl 1 rnd, knit 1 rnd, purl 1 rnd.

BO all sts loosely.

SLEEVES

Sl 56 (64, 66, 72, 82) sleeve sts on larger 16"-long needle, CO 7 (7, 10, 10, 10) sts at beg, knit to end, CO 7 (7, 10, 10, 10) sts—70 (78, 86, 92, 102) sts. Pm, join in the rnd.

K2tog on each side of marker every 6th row 11 times—48 (56, 64, 70, 80) sts.

Work even until sleeve measures 13".

Change to smaller 16"-long needle. Work 3 rnds in garter st.

BO all sts loosely.

NECKBAND

With RS facing you and smaller 16"-long needle, attach yarn at left shoulder, *PU 1 st in next 3 sts, sk next st, rep from * around neck. Pm, join in the rnd. Work 3 rnds in garter st. BO all sts loosely.

FINISHING

Sew underarm seams. Weave in ends.

SETUP

Garment is worked from the neck down.

With larger needle, CO 54 (56, 58, 74, 74) sts. Do not join in the rnd.

Setup row: K1 (neck edge), pm twice, K1 (sleeve seam st), pm, K10 (10, 10, 14, 14) (sleeve sts), pm, K1 (sleeve seam st), pm, K28 (30, 32, 40, 40) (back sts), pm, K1 (sleeve seam st), pm, K10 (10, 10, 14, 14) (sleeve sts), pm, K1 (sleeve seam st), pm twice, K1, turn.

Next row: Purl, slipping markers as you come to them.

NECK AND RAGLAN INCS

Inc row: K1, slip marker, M1 twice, sl marker, K1, sl marker, M1, (knit to next marker, M1, sl marker, K1, sl marker, M1) 3 times, end M1, sl marker, K1. Note that first and last sts are the neck edge. The first inc row is the only time you will make two M1s in a row.

Double Diamond

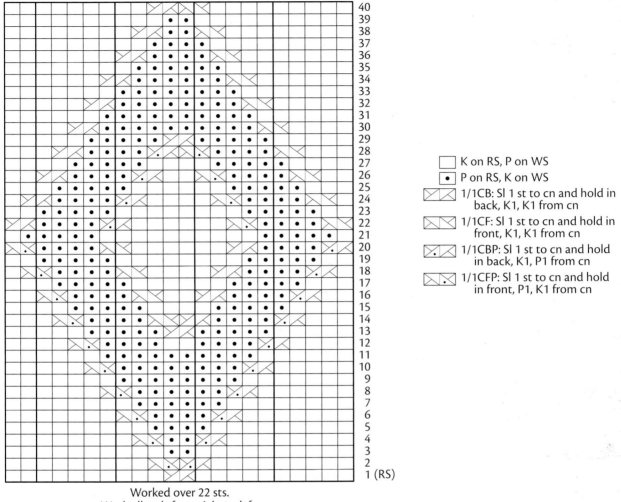

40
39
38
37
36
35
34
33
32
31
30
29
28
27
26
25
24
23
22
21
20
19
18
17
16
15
14
13
12
11
10
9
8
7
6
5
4
3
2
1 (RS)

Worked over 22 sts.
Work all rnds from right to left.

	K on RS, P on WS
•	P on RS, K on WS
	1/1CB: Sl 1 st to cn and hold in back, K1, K1 from cn
	1/1CF: Sl 1 st to cn and hold in front, K1, K1 from cn
	1/1CBP: Sl 1 st to cn and hold in back, K1, P1 from cn
	1/1CFP: Sl 1 st to cn and hold in front, P1, K1 from cn

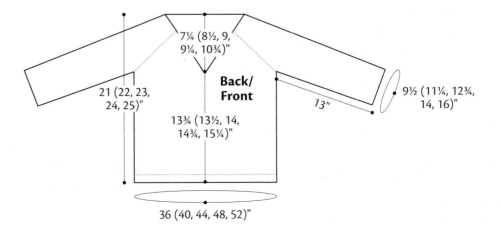

7¼ (8½, 9, 9¼, 10¾)"

Back/Front

21 (22, 23, 24, 25)"

13"

9½ (11¼, 12¾, 14, 16)"

13¾ (13½, 14, 14¾, 15¼)"

36 (40, 44, 48, 52)"

Susie

This colorful sweater is perfect for the weekend— slightly oversized and definitely cheerful!

Sizes: S (M, L, XL, 2X)

Finished Bust: 38 (42, 46, 50, 54)"

Finished Length: 22 (23, 24, 25, 26)"

MATERIALS

Sierra from Cascade Yarns (80% pima cotton, 20% wool; 100 g/3.5 oz; 174 m/191 yds) ◼

MC 4 (5, 5, 6, 6) skeins in color 66 navy

A   2 (2, 3, 3, 3) skeins in color 400 lime

B   1 skein in color 39 burgundy

C   1 skein in color 55 coral

D   1 skein in color 44 periwinkle

Size 5 (3.75 mm) circular needles (16" and 32" long)

Size 7 (4.5 mm) circular needles (16" and 32" long)

2 stitch holders

Waste yarn for provisional cast on

1 stitch marker

1 detachable marker or safety pin

Tapestry needle

Gauge: 19 sts and 26 rows = 4" in St st with larger needle

BACK

Back is worked from shoulders down.

With larger 32"-long needle and waste yarn, use provisional CO (see page 8) to CO 90 (100, 110, 118, 128) sts. Do not join in the rnd. Using A, PU sts into provisional CO and work in St st for 7½ (8, 8½, 9, 9½)". Place sts on holder.

FRONT

Front is worked from shoulders down.

Beg at left shoulder, unravel first 30 (33, 36, 39, 42) sts from provisional CO, place sts on larger 32"-long needle, unravel center 30 (34, 38, 40, 44) sts and place on holder, unravel rem 30 (33, 36, 39, 42) sts and place on needle. Place detachable marker, work both sides with separate yarn balls in St st for 10 rows.

SHAPE NECK

With RS facing you, work in St st, inc 1 st at each neck edge (either knit inc or purl inc) every row 5 times—35 (38, 41, 44, 47) sts each side.

Next row: Work to center, CO (see "Cable Cast On" on page 8) 20 (24, 28, 30, 34) sts, work to end. You now only need 1 ball of yarn. Cont in St st until piece measures 7½ (8, 8½, 9, 9½)" from marker.

BODY

With RS facing you and MC, pm and join front and back sts in the rnd. Work in St st until piece measures 13½ (14, 14½, 15, 15½)" from bottom of armhole. Change to smaller 32"-long needle and work in garter st (purl 1 rnd, knit 1 rnd) for 1". BO all sts loosely.

SLEEVES

With RS facing you, larger 16"-long needle, and beg at undearm with MC, PU 72 (76, 80, 84, 88) sts. Pm, join in the rnd. Work 12 rnds of MC.

Dec rnd: K2tog, knit to 2 sts before marker, K2tog.

Work color sequence as follows and AT THE SAME TIME work dec rnd every 6th row a total of 14 times—44 (48, 52, 56, 60) sts.

6 rnds of MC

9 rnds in B

9 rnds in A

9 rnds in MC

9 rnds in C

9 rnds in A

9 rnds in MC

9 rnds in D

9 rnds in A

9 rnds in MC

Sleeve should measure approx 16".

Cuff: Change to smaller 16"-long needle and work as follows:

> **Rnd 1:** With MC, purl.
>
> **Rnd 2:** With A, knit.
>
> Rep rnds 1 and 2 three more times, then work rnd 1 once (9 rnds total). With A, loosely BO all sts knitwise.

NECKBAND

With RS facing you and smaller 16"-long needle, attach MC. Beg at left shoulder, PU 76 (80, 84, 88, 92) sts, pm, join in the rnd. Work in garter st as for cuff.

Weave in ends.

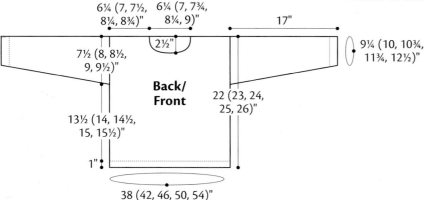

6¼ (7, 7½, 8¼, 8¾)"   6¼ (7, 7¾, 8¼, 9)"   17"

2½"

7½ (8, 8½, 9, 9½)"

9¼ (10, 10¾, 11¾, 12½)"

Back/Front

22 (23, 24, 25, 26)"

13½ (14, 14½, 15, 15½)"

1"

38 (42, 46, 50, 54)"

I designed this Aran-style sweater about 25 years ago. Back then, it was made in pieces and sewn together. This is a seamless remake. Classic cable work never goes out of style.

Kimberly

Skill Level: Experienced ◼◼◼◼▶

Sizes: S (M, L, XL, 2X)

Finished Bust: 36 (40, 44, 48, 52)"

Finished Length: 20 (21, 22, 23, 24)"

MATERIALS

10 (11, 12, 13, 14) skeins of Jeannee from Plymouth Yarn (51% cotton, 49% acrylic; 50 g/1.75 oz; 101 m/111 yds) in color 2 salmon (4)

Size 5 (3.75 mm) circular needles (16" and 32" long) and double-pointed needles

Size 7 (4.5 mm) circular needles (16" and 32" long)

1 stitch marker

2 stitch holders

Waste yarn for provisional cast on

1 detachable stitch marker or safety pin

Cable needle

Tapestry needle

Gauge: 20 sts and 25 rows = 4" in St st with larger needle

PATTERN STITCHES

3/3CF: Sl 3 sts to cn and hold in front, K3, K3 from cn.

3/3CB: Sl 3 sts to cn and hold in back, K3, K3 from cn.

Left Cable

(Worked over 6 sts)

Back and forth:

Rows 1 and 5: K6.

Rows 2 and 4: P6.

Row 3: Work 3/3CF.

Row 6. P6.

Rep rows 1–6 for patt.

In the round:

Rnds 1, 2, 4, and 5: K6.

Rnd 3: Work 3/3CF.

Rnd 6: K6.

Rep rnds 1–6 for patt.

Right Cable

(Worked over 6 sts)

Back and forth:

Rows 1 and 5: K6.

Rows 2 and 4: P6.

Row 3: Work 3/3CB.

Row 6: P6.

Rep rows 1–6 for patt.

In the round:

Rnds 1, 2, 4, and 5: K6.

Rnd 3: Work 3/3CB.

Rnd 6: K6.

Rep rnds 1–6 for patt.

4-st Rib

(Worked over 4 sts)

Back and forth:

Row 1: Knit.

Row 2: P1, *K2, P2; rep from * to last 3 sts, K2, P1.

Rep rows 1 and 2 for patt.

In the round:

Row 1: Knit.

Row 2: K1, *P2, K2; rep to last 3 sts, P2, K1.

Rep rows 1 and 2 for patt.

Reverse Stockinette Stitch

(Worked over any number of sts)

Back and forth:

Row 1 (RS): Purl.

Row 2: Knit.

Rep rows 1 and 2 for patt.

In the round:

Every rnd: Purl.

Small Diamond

See chart on page 57 or follow written instructions below.

(Worked over 15 sts)

Row 1: P7, K1, P7.

Row 2 and all even-numbered rows: Knit the knit sts and purl the purl sts as they face you.

Row 3: P6, K3, P6.

Row 5: P5, K5, P5.

Row 7: P4, K3, P1, K3, P4.

Row 9: P3, K3, P3, K3, P3.

Row 11: P2, K3, P5, K3, P2.

Row 13: P1, K3, P7, K3, P1.

Row 15: K3, P9, K3.

Row 17: P1, K3, P7, K3, P1.

Row 19: K1, P1, K3, P5, K3, P1, K1.

Row 21: K2, P1, K3, P3, K3, P1, K2.

Row 23: K3, P1, K3, P1, K3, P1, K3.

Row 25: K4, P1, K5, P1, K4.

Row 27: K5, P1, K3, P1, K5.

Row 29: K6, P1, K1, P1, K6.

Row 31: K6, P3, K6.

Row 32: Knit the knit sts and purl the purl sts as they face you.

Rep rows 1–32 for patt.

Large Diamond

See chart on page 57 or follow written instructions below. When working back and forth from written instructions, work rows as given. When working in the rnd from written instructions, work all rows (which will be rnds) from right to left.

(Worked over 25 sts)

Row 1: P12, K1, P12.

Row 2 and all even-numbered rows: Knit the knit sts and purl the purl sts as they face you.

Row 3: P11, K3, P11.

Row 5: P10, K5, P10.

Row 7: P9, K7, P9.

Row 9: P8, K9, P8.

Row 11: P7, K5, P1, K5, P7.

Row 13: P6, K5, P3, K5, P6.

Row 15: P5, K5, P5, K5, P5.

Row 17: P4, K5, P7, K5, P4.

Row 19: P3, K5, P9, K5, P3.

Row 21: P2, K5, P11, K5, P2.

Row 23: P1, K5, P13, K5, P1.

Row 25: K5, P15, K5.

Row 27: Rep row 23.

Row 29: Rep row 21.

Row 31: Rep row 19.

Row 33: Rep row 17.

Row 35: Rep row 15.

Row 37: Rep row 13.

Row 39: Rep row 11.

Row 41: Rep row 9.

Row 43: Rep row 7.

Row 45: Rep row 5.

Row 47: Rep row 3.

Row 48: Knit the knit sts and purl the purl sts as they face you.

Rep rows 1–48 twice.

BACK

Back is worked from shoulder down.

With larger 32"-long needle and waste yarn, use provisional CO (see page 8) to CO 90 (100, 110, 120, 130) sts. Do not join in the rnd. Using main yarn, PU sts into provisional CO and work in St st for 7½ (8, 8½, 9, 9½)". Place sts on holder.

FRONT

Front is worked from shoulders down.

Beg at left shoulder of back, unravel 29 (32, 36, 40, 45) sts from CO and place on larger 32"-long needle, unravel center 32 (36, 38, 40, 40) sts from CO and place on st holder, unravel rem 29 (32, 36, 40, 45) sts from CO and place on needle. Place detachable marker, work both sides with separate yarn balls in St st for 2 rows.

Shape neck: On next RS row, work setup row below. AT THE SAME TIME inc 1 st at each side of neck EOR 7 (7, 9, 10, 10) times.

Setup Row

Note that not all sts exist in the setup patt. Work as many patt sts adjacent to the neck as you can. Once increases are done, the patts will be complete as written. Work the right and left shoulders in established patt, and all new sts at neck in rev St st.

Work as follows and AT THE SAME TIME work incs as above:

Left shoulder: Beg at side edge, work 5 (8, 11, 14, 17) sts in St st, pm, work 2 sts in rev St st, pm, work 15 sts in small diamond, pm, work 4 (5, 6, 7, 8) sts in rev St st, pm, work 4 sts in 4-st rib, pm, work 4 (5, 6, 7, 8) sts in rev St st.

Right shoulder: Beg at neck edge, work 4 (5, 6, 7, 8) sts in rev St st, pm, work 4 sts in 4-st rib, pm, work 4 (5, 6, 7, 8) sts in rev St st, pm, work 15 sts in small diamond, pm, work 2 sts in rev St st and 5 (6, 8, 11, 14, 17) sts in St st.

Join Left and Right Fronts

After all incs are done, work in patt to center, CO (see page 8) 21 (25, 23, 23, 23) sts, work in patt to end. You now only need one ball of yarn.

Work 4 (6, 8, 10, 10) rows in patt, with newly CO center sts in rev St st.

On next RS row, work 34 (39, 44, 49, 54) sts in patt and 25 sts in large diamond, work in patt to end.

Cont in patt and, when small diamond chart is complete, work those 15 sts on each side as right cable, 3 sts in rev St st, left cable. Work in patt until front piece measures 7½ (8, 8½, 9, 9½)".

BODY

Pm, join in the rnd. Work back sts in St st and front sts in patt until large diamond chart has been worked twice. Cont in St st until total length is 17½ (18½, 19½, 20½, 21½)".

Dec 3 sts evenly on last rnd—180 (200, 220, 240, 260) sts.

Change to smaller 32"-long needle, work in K2, P2 ribbing for 2½".

BO all sts in patt loosely.

SLEEVES

With RS facing you, larger 16"-long needle, and beg at underarm, PU 76 (80, 86, 90, 96) sts, pm, and join in the rnd. Work in St st for 1½".

Dec rnd: K2tog, work to last 2 sts, K2tog. Work dec rnd every 6th rnd a total of 15 times—46 (50, 56, 60, 66) sts.

Work even until sleeve measures 15 (15½, 15½, 15½, 15½)"; dec 2 (2, 4, 8 14) sts evenly on last rnd—44 (48, 52, 52, 52) sts.

Change to dpns, work K2, P2 ribbing for 2½".

BO all sts in patt loosely.

NECKBAND

With RS facing you, smaller 32"-long needle, and beg at left shoulder, PU 80 (84, 88, 92, 96) sts evenly around neck, including back sts from holder. Work in K2, P2 ribbing for 2½". BO all sts in patt loosely.

Weave in ends.

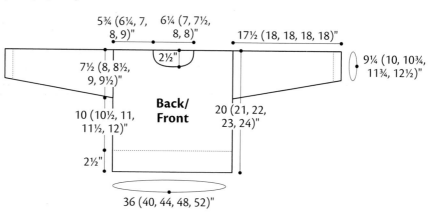

Small Diamond

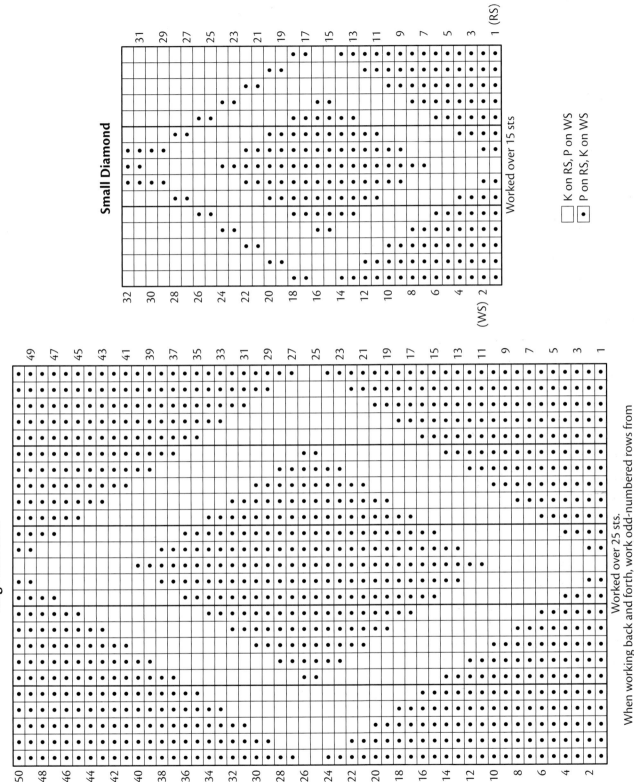

Worked over 15 sts

Large Diamond

Worked over 25 sts.
When working back and forth, work odd-numbered rows from right to left and even-numbered rows from left to right.
When working in the rnd, work all rnds from right to left.

☐ K on RS, P on WS
● P on RS, K on WS

Paula

Simple texture always adds great style to a sweater. Using a bulky yarn makes for wonderfully cozy winter attire.

Sizes: S (M, L, XL 2XL)

Finished Bust: 36 (40, 44, 48, 52)"

Finished Length: 20 (21, 22, 23, 24)"

MATERIALS

9 (10, 11, 12, 13) skeins of Venezia from Cascade Yarns (70% merino wool, 30% silk; 100 g/3.5 oz; 93 m/102 yds) in color 107 purple (5)

Size 8 (5 mm) circular needles (16" and 32" long)

Size 10 (6 mm) circular needles (16" and 32" long)

Waste yarn for provisional cast on

1 stitch marker

2 stitch holders

1 detachable stitch marker or safety pin

Tapestry needle

Gauge: 14 sts and 20 rows = 4" in St st with larger needle

PATTERN STITCHES

Seed Stitch Rib

(Worked over 8 sts)

Rnd 1: *K1, P2 (K1, P1) twice, P1; rep from * around.

Rnd 2: *K1, P1; rep from * around.

Reps rnds 1 and 2 for patt.

Seed Stitch Center Panel

See chart on page 60 or follow written instructions below.

(Worked over 17 sts)

Back and forth:

Row 1: P1, K1, P2, K9, P2, K1, P1.

Row 2: (K1, P1) twice, K1, P7, (K1, P1) twice, K1.

Row 3: P1, K1, P2, K1, P1, K5, P1, K1, P2, K1, P1.

Row 4: (K1, P1) 3 times, K1, P3, (K1, P1) 3 times, K1.

Rows 5, 7, and 9: P1, K1, P2, (K1, P1) 4 times, K1, P2, K1, P1.

Rows 6, 8, and 10: (K1, P1) 8 times, K1.

Row 11: P1, K1, P1, K2, (P1, K1) 3 times, P1, K2, P1, K1, P1.

Row 12: K1, P1, K1, P3, (K1, P1) twice, K1, P3, K1, P1, K1.

Row 13: P1, K1, P1, K4, P1, K1, P1, K4, P1, K1, P1.

Row 14: K1, P1, K1, P5, K1, P5, K1, P1, K1.

Rep rows 1–14 for patt.

In the round:

Rnd 1: P1, K1, P2, K9, P2, K1, P1.

Rnd 2: (P1, K1) twice, P1, K7, (P1, K1) twice, P1.

Rnd 3: P1, K1, P2, K1, P1, K5, P1, K1, P2, K1, P1.

Rnd 4: (P1, K1) 3 times, P1, K3, (P1, K1) 3 times, P1.

Rnds 5, 7, and 9: P1, K1, P2, (K1, P1) 4 times, K1, P2, K1, P1.

Rnds 6, 8, and 10: (P1, K1) 8 times, P1.

Rnd 11: P1, K1, P1, K2, (P1, K1) 3 times, P1, K2, P1, K1, P1.

Rnd 12: P1, K1, P1, K3, (P1, K1) twice, P1, K3, P1, K1, P1.

Rnd 13: P1, K1, P1, K4, P1, K1, P1, K4, P1, K1, P1.

Rnd 14: P1, K1, P1, K5, P1, K5, P1, K1, P1.

Rep rnds 1–14 for patt.

BACK

Back is worked from shoulder down.

With larger 32"-long needle and waste yarn, use provisional CO (see page 8) to CO 63 (71, 77, 85, 91) sts. Do not join in the rnd. Using main yarn, PU sts into provisional CO and work in St st for 8 (8½, 9, 9½, 10)". Place sts on holder.

FRONT

Front is worked from shoulders down.

Beg at left shoulder on back, unravel first 20 (23, 25, 28, 31) sts from CO, place sts on larger 32"-long needle, unravel center 23 (25, 27, 29, 29) sts and place on st holder, unravel rem 20 (23, 25,28, 31) sts and place on needle. (RS) Place detachable marker, work both sides with separate yarn balls in St st for 4 rows.

Shape neck: On next RS row, working in St st, inc 1 st at each edge EOR 6 (6, 7, 7, 7) times—63 (71, 77, 85, 91) sts. On next WS row, work to neck edge, CO 11 (13, 13, 15, 15) sts, work to end. You now only need one ball of yarn.

On next RS row, work 23 (27, 30, 34, 37) sts in St st, work seed st center panel back and forth over next 17 sts, work 23 (27, 30, 34, 37) sts in St st. Cont until piece measures 8 (8½, 9, 9½, 10)" from detachable marker.

BODY

Pm, join in the rnd, work back sts in St st and front sts in patt until piece measures 18 (19, 20, 21, 22)". Dec 6 (6, 2, 2, 6) sts evenly on last rnd—120 (136, 152, 168, 176) sts.

Change to smaller 32"-long needle and work seed st rib for 2". BO all sts in patt loosely.

SLEEVES

With RS facing you, larger 16"-long needle, and beg at underarm, PU 58 (60, 64, 68, 70) sts. Pm, join in the rnd. Work in St st for 8 rnds.

Dec rnd: K2tog, work to last 2 sts, K2tog.

Work dec rnd every 5th rnd a total of 13 times—32 (34, 38, 42, 44) sts. Work even until sleeve measures 15½ (16, 16, 16, 16)"; dec 0 (2, 6, 2, 4) sts evenly in last rnd—32 (32, 32, 40, 40) sts.

Switch to dpns and work seed st rib for 2". BO all sts in patt loosely.

NECKBAND

With RS facing you, smaller 16"-long needle, and beg at left shoulder, PU 56 (56, 64, 64, 64) sts, including back sts on holder. Pm, join in the rnd, work seed st rib for 2". BO all sts in patt loosely.

Weave in ends.

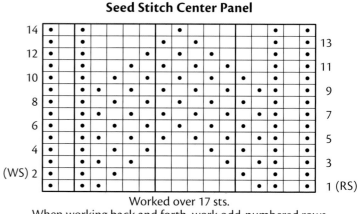

Seed Stitch Center Panel

Worked over 17 sts.
When working back and forth, work odd-numbered rows from right to left, and even-numbered rows from left to right.
When working in the rnd, work all rnds from right to left.

☐ K on RS, P on WS
▪ P on RS, K on WS

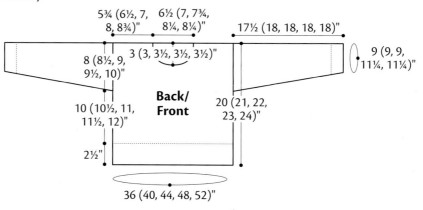

5¾ (6½, 7, 8, 8¾)"

6½ (7, 7¾, 8¼, 8¼)"

17½ (18, 18, 18, 18)"

8 (8½, 9, 9½, 10)"

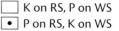
3 (3, 3½, 3½, 3½)"

9 (9, 9, 11¼, 11¼)"

Back/Front

20 (21, 22, 23, 24)"

10 (10½, 11, 11½, 12)"

2½"

36 (40, 44, 48, 52)"

SOMEWHAT
SIDE TO SIDE

Last but not least, the designs in this section are made somewhat side to side, not too challenging, but with a different approach to making a garment. These are my favorite styles; it seems to break up the normal way of making a garment.

Perri

This is an easy-knitting, tunic-length vest with just a little seaming involved at the shoulders and collar.

Sizes: S (M, L, XL, 2XL)

Finished Bust: 40 (44, 48, 52, 56)"

Finished Length: 21½ (22, 23, 24, 25)"

MATERIALS

6 (7, 8, 9, 10) skeins of Fresco from Wisdom Yarns (100% cotton; 50 g/1.75 oz; 100 m/109 yds) in color 1619 ❸

Size 7 (4.5 mm) straight or circular needle (32" long)

Tapestry needle

Gauge: 17 sts (slightly stretched) and 30 rows = 4" in garter st

PATTERN STITCH

Every row: Sl1p wyif, knit to end.

VEST

Vest is worked side to side, beg with collar on right front. I use the provisional CO method (page 8) because it leaves a nice edge.

Right collar: Use project yarn and provisional CO to CO 106 (110, 116, 123, 129) sts. Work in patt until piece measures 4½ (5, 5½, 6, 6½)", ending with completed WS row.

Shape shoulder: BO 15 (17, 19, 21, 23) sts at beg of next row. Cont in patt for 4 (4½, 5, 5½, 6)", ending with completed WS row.

Shape armhole: BO 32 (34, 36, 38, 40) sts at beg of next row. Cont in patt for 4", ending with completed WS row.

Shape back: Use cable CO (see page 8) to CO 32 (34, 36, 38, 40) sts at beg of next row. Cont in patt for 15 (17, 19, 21, 23)", ending with completed WS row.

Shape armhole: BO 32 (34, 36, 38, 40) sts at beg of next row. Cont in patt for 4", ending with completed WS row.

Shape shoulder: CO 32 (34, 36, 38, 40) sts at beg of next row. Cont in patt for 4 (4½, 5, 5½, 6)", ending with completed WS row.

Left collar: CO 15 (17, 19, 21, 23) sts at beg of next row. Cont in patt for 4½ (5, 5½, 6, 6½)" ending with completed WS row. BO loosely.

FINISHING

Fold vest, matching front and back shoulders, and sew shoulder seams. Sew ends of collar tog from inside and fold over. Weave in ends.

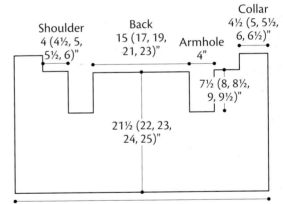

Shoulder 4 (4½, 5, 5½, 6)"

Back 15 (17, 19, 21, 23)"

Collar 4½ (5, 5½, 6, 6½)"

Armhole 4"

7½ (8, 8½, 9, 9½)"

21½ (22, 23, 24, 25)"

40 (44, 48, 52, 56)"

Riana is perfect for bringing out your feminine side. The cotton/silk combination allows the edge of the sleeve and waist to drape nicely.

Riana

Skill Level: Intermediate ■■■□

Sizes: S (M, L, XL, 2XL)

Finished Bust: 36 (40, 44, 48, 52)"

Finished Length: 20 (21, 22, 23, 24)"

MATERIALS

6 (7, 8, 9, 10) skeins of Pima Silk from Frog Tree (85% pima cotton, 15% silk; 50 g/1.75 oz; 141 m/155 yds) in color 801 natural ❷

Size 6 (4 mm) circular needles (16" and 32" long)

Size E-4 (3.5 mm) crochet hook

2 stitch holders

1 stitch marker

Tapestry needle

Gauge: 22 and 30 sts = 4" in St st

DIAMOND PATTERN

See chart on page 66 or follow written instructions below.

(Multiple of 12 + 3 sts)

Row 1: K2, (K5, P1, K6) 5 times, K1.

Row 2: P1, (P5, K3, P4) 5 times, P2.

Row 3: K2, (K3, P5, K4) 5 times, K1.

Row 4: P1, (P3, K7, P2) 5 times, P2.

Row 5: K2, (K1, P9, K2) 5 times, K1.

Row 6: P1, (P1, K11) 5 times, P2.

Row 7: Rep row 5.

Row 8: Rep row 4.

Row 9: Rep row 3.

Row 10: Rep row 2.

Rep rows 1–10 for patt.

BACK PANEL

With 32"-long needle, CO 63 sts. Purl 1 row. Work in diamond patt until piece measures 19 (20, 21, 22, 23)", ending with completed RS row. Work in patt over 15 (14, 12, 10, 8) sts, BO center 33 (35, 39, 43, 47) sts, work to end. Place shoulder sts on holders.

FRONT PANEL

Work as for back until piece measures 17½ (18½, 19½, 20½, 21½)", ending with completed WS row.

Shape neck: Work in patt over 25 (24, 22, 20, 18) sts, attach a new ball of yarn, BO center 13 (15, 19, 23, 27) sts, work rem 25 (24, 22, 20, 18) sts. Dec 1 st (either K2tog or P2tog) each side of neck edge every row 10 times—15 (14, 12, 10, 8) sts.

Work even in patt until piece measures 20 (21, 22, 23, 24)", ending with completed WS row.

Sew shoulders: Place back shoulder sts on needles. With RS facing tog, join front and back shoulders using 3-needle BO (see page 8).

RIGHT SIDE GUSSET

With RS facing you, 32"-long needle, and beg at lower back, PU 110 (115, 121, 126, 132) sts to shoulder, PU 110 (115, 121, 126, 132) sts from shoulder to lower front—220 (230, 242, 252, 264) sts. Do not join in the rnd. Work 3 rows in garter st. Work in St st until gusset measures 3 (4, 5, 6, 7)", ending with completed WS row.

SLEEVES

Bring tips of needles tog so that RS are tog. Join first and last 71 (69, 70, 70, 71) sts using 3-needle BO. Fasten off but do not cut yarn. Turn work to RS. Using 16"-long needle, PU 1 st at seam, work 78 (88, 98, 108, 118) sts, PU 1 st at seam—80 (90, 100, 110, 120) sts. Pm, join in the rnd. Work in St st for 2". Work 3 rnds in garter st.

Cuff: Work picot edge as follows:

Row 1: K2tog, *return st from RH to LH needle, CO 2 sts (see "Cable Cast On" on page 8), K2, K2tog, turn.

Row 2: K3, turn.

Row 3: K1, M1, K1, K2tog, turn.

Row 4: K4, turn.

Row 5: K1, M1, K2, K2tog, turn.

Row 6: K5, turn.

Row 7: K1, M1, K3, K2tog, turn.

Row 8: K6, turn.

Row 9: K1, ssk, K2, K2tog, turn.

Row 10: K5, turn.

Row 11: K1, ssk, K1, K2tog, turn.

Row 12: K4, turn.

Row 13: K1, ssk, K2tog, turn.

Row 14: K3, turn.

Row 15: Work decs and BO as follows: K1, ssk, BO 1 st, K1, BO 2 sts.*

Rep from * to * a total of 8 (9, 10, 11, 12) times.

On last row of last rep, end K1, ssk, BO 1 st , K1, BO 1 st, K1, BO 1 st. Fasten off.

LEFT SIDE GUSSET

Rep right side gusset through sleeve except PU beg from lower front to shoulder, then from shoulder to lower back.

BOTTOM BAND

With RS facing and 32"-long needle, PU 200 (220, 240, 260, 280) sts. Pm, join in the rnd. Purl 1 rnd, knit 1 rnd, purl 1 rnd. Work rows 1–15 of picot edge a total of 20 (22, 24, 26, 28) times. Fasten off.

NECKBAND

With RS facing you, attach yarn at left neck edge and work 1 rnd of sc.

Next rnd: Work (4 sc, ch 3) around. Fasten off.

Weave in ends.

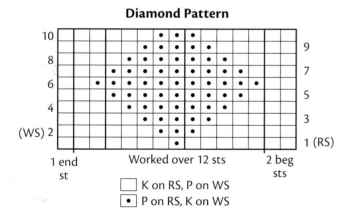

Diamond Pattern

1 end st — Worked over 12 sts — 2 beg sts

☐ K on RS, P on WS
▪ P on RS, K on WS

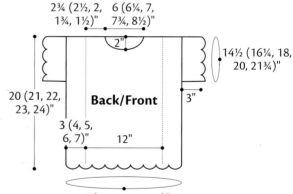

2¾ (2½, 2, 1¾, 1½)"   6 (6¼, 7, 7¾, 8½)"

2"

14½ (16¼, 18, 20, 21¾)"

20 (21, 22, 23, 24)"   **Back/Front**   3"

3 (4, 5, 6, 7)"   12"

36 (40, 44, 48, 52)"

Intriguing entrelac! Follow the simple steps and soon you'll be on your way to wearing this alluring design. When making the entrelac panels, be sure to write down what row you are on when you decide to take a break, so that you can easily find your place when you pick up your needles again.

Jackie

Skill Level: Intermediate ◀■■□

Sizes: S (M, L, XL, 2XL)

Finished Bust: 38 (42, 46, 50, 54)"

Finished Length: 21 (21, 25, 25, 25)"

MATERIALS

7 (8, 10, 11, 12) skeins of Taos from Crystal Palace Yarns (100% wool; 50 g/1.75 oz; 118 m/128 yds) in color 18 Mineral ④

Size 7 (4.5 mm) circular needles (16" and 32" long)

Size 9 (5.5 mm) circular needles (16" and 32" long)

2 stitch markers

Tapestry needle

Gauge: 16 sts and 20 rows = 4" in St st with larger needle

ENTRELAC PANELS (MAKE 2.)

Entrelac panels are worked from bottom to neck, beg with bottom triangles.

Step 1: Bottom Triangles

With larger 32"-long needle, CO 40 sts, pm after 10th, 20th, and 30th st.

Row 1 (WS): P2, turn.

Row 2: K2, turn.

Row 3: P3, turn.

Row 4: K3, turn.

Row 5: P4, turn.

Row 6: K4, turn.

Row 7: P5, turn.

Row 8: K5, turn.

Row 9: P6, turn.

Row 10: K6, turn.

Row 11: P7, turn.

Row 12: K7, turn.

Row 13: P8, turn.

Row 14: K8, turn.

Row 15: P9, turn.

Row 16: K9, turn.

Row 17: P10. Leave 10 sts on RH needle. Do not turn, sl marker.

Rep from row 1, leaving 10 sts in each group on RH needle when completed, until all 40 sts have been worked—4 triangles completed. Remove markers.

Step 2: Right-Edge Triangle

Row 1 (RS): K2, turn.

Row 2: P2, turn.

Row 3: K1, M1, ssk , turn.

Row 4: P3, turn.

Row 5: K1, M1, K1, ssk, turn.

Row 6: P4, turn.

Row 7: K1, M1, K2, ssk, turn.

Row 8: P5, turn.

Row 9: K1, M1, K3, ssk, turn.

Row 10: P6, turn.

Row 11: K1, M1, K4, ssk, turn.

Row 12: P7, turn.

Row 13: K1, M1, K5, ssk, turn.

Row 14: P8, turn.

Row 15: K1, M1, K6, ssk, turn.

Row 16: P9, turn.

Row 17: K1, M1, K7, ssk—10 sts on RH needle.

Rep rows 1–17 for each right-edge triangle.

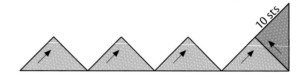

Step 3: Left-Slant Rectangle

*With RS facing you, PU 10 sts evenly along side of triangle (or rectangle), turn.

Row 1 (WS): P10, turn.

Row 2: K9, ssk, turn.

Rep rows 1 and 2 until all sts of previous triangle (or rectangle) have been worked into new rectangle.

Rep from * to make 2 more left-slant rectangles.

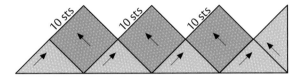

Step 4: Left-Edge Triangle

With RS facing you, PU 10 sts evenly along side of triangle (or rectangle), turn.

Row 1 (WS): P2tog, P8, turn.

Row 2: K9, turn.

Row 3: P2tog, P7, turn.

Row 4: K8, turn.

Row 5: P2tog, P6, turn.

Row 6: K7, turn.

Row 7: P2tog, P5, turn.

Row 8: K6, turn.

Row 9: P2tog, P4, turn.

Row 10: K5, turn.

Row 11: P2tog, P3, turn.

Row 12: K4, turn.

Row 13: P2tog, P2, turn.

Row 14: K3, turn.

Row 15: P2tog, P1, turn.

Row 16: K2, turn.

Row 17: P2tog. Do not turn—1 st rem.

Work rows 1–17 for each left-edge triangle.

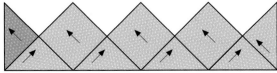

Step 5: Right-Slant Rectangle

*With WS facing you, PU 9 sts purlwise, turn—10 sts.

Row 1 (RS): K10, turn.

Row 2: P9, P2tog, turn.

Rep rows 1 and 2 until all sts of previous triangle (or rectangle) have been worked into new rectangle. Do not turn after finishing last row.

Rep from * to make 3 more right-slant rectangles.

Rep steps 2–5 another 2 (2, 3, 3, 3) times, then rep steps 2–4 once more.

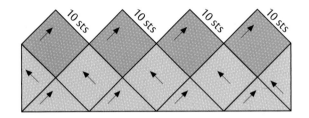

Step 6: Top Triangle

With WS facing, PU 10 sts purlwise evenly along previous rectangle, turn—11 sts.

Row 1 (RS): K9, ssk, turn.

Row 2: P9, P2tog, turn.

Row 3: K8, ssk, turn.

Row 4: P8, P2tog, turn.

Row 5: K7, ssk, turn.

Row 6: P7, P2tog, turn.

Row 7: K6, ssk, turn.

Row 8: P6, P2tog, turn.

Row 9: K5, ssk, turn.

Row 10: P5, P2tog, turn.

Row 11: K4, ssk, turn.

Row 12: P4, P2tog, turn.

Row 13: K3, ssk, turn.

Row 14: P3, P2tog, turn.

Row 15: K2, ssk, turn.

Row 16: P2, P2tog, turn.

Row 17: K1, ssk, turn.

Row 18: P1, P2tog, turn.

Row 19: Ssk, turn.

Row 20: P2tog; do not turn.

Rep rows 1–20 three more times. Fasten off.

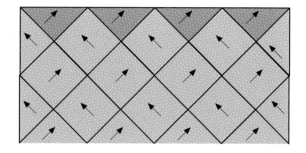

Sew shoulders: Mark center 8½ (9, 9½, 10, 10½)" for neck opening on front and back entrelac panels. With RS facing tog and larger needle, join front and back shoulders tog using 3-needle BO (see page 8).

RIGHT SIDE GUSSET

With RS facing you, 32"-long needle, and beg at lower edge of back, PU 82 (82, 98, 98, 98) sts along side edge to shoulder, then 82 (82, 98, 98, 98) sts along side edge from shoulder down—164 (164, 196, 196, 196) sts.

Work 3 rows in garter st. Change to St st and work for 2 (3, 4, 5, 6)", ending with completed WS row.

SLEEVES

Bring tips of needle tog so that RS are tog. Join first and last 52 (50, 65, 63, 61) sts using 3-needle BO. Fasten off but do not cut yarn. Turn work to RS. Using larger 16"-long needle, PU 1 st at seam, work 60 (64, 66, 70, 74) rem sts, PU 1 st at seam—62 (66, 68, 72, 76) sts. Pm, join in the rnd.

Work in St st for 10 rnds.

Dec rnd: K2tog after marker, knit to last 2 sts before marker, K2tog. Rep dec every 6th rnd 12 more times—36 (40, 42, 46, 50) sts.

Work even until sleeve measures 15 (15½, 15½, 15, 15)".

Change to smaller 16"-long needle and work in garter st (purl 1 rnd, knit 1 rnd) for 2½". BO all sts loosely.

LEFT SIDE GUSSET

Work as for right side gusset except PU from lower front to shoulder, then from shoulder to lower back.

Work second sleeve as first sleeve.

BOTTOM BAND

With RS facing you, smaller 32"-long needle, and beg at left-front bottom edge, PU 128 (144, 160, 176, 192) sts. Pm, join in the rnd. Work in garter st for 2½". BO all sts loosely.

COLLAR

With RS facing you, smaller 16"-long needle, and beg at left front, PU 64 (72, 80, 88, 96) sts. Pm, join in the rnd. Work in garter st for 2½". BO all sts loosely.

Weave in ends.

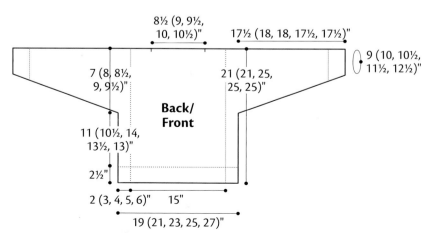

JACKIE

This casual sweater is knit from a self-striping yarn. It's fun to knit, and the yarn does all the color work! If stripes aren't your thing, this pattern looks great in a solid color, too.

Wendy

Sizes: S (M, L, XL, 2XL)

Finished Bust: 36 (40, 44, 48, 52)"

Finished Length: 22 (23, 24, 25, 26)"

MATERIALS

9 (10, 11, 12, 13) skeins of Sonnet from Wisdom Yarns (75% wool, 25% silk; 50 g/1.75 oz; 85 m/93 yds) in color 715 Autumn [4]

Size 6 (4 mm) circular needles (16" and 32" long)

Size 8 (5 mm) circular needles (16" and 32" long)

1 stitch marker

3 stitch holders

Tapestry needle

Gauge: 17 sts and 24 rows = 4" in St st with larger needle

BASKET WEAVE PATTERN

(Worked over 44 sts)

Rows 1, 3, and 5: K2, (K5, P5) 4 times, K2.

Rows 2, 4, and 6: P2, (K5, P5) 4 times, P2.

Rows 7, 9, and 11: K2, (P5, K5) 4 times, K2.

Rows 8, 10, and 12: P2, (P5, K5) 4 times, P2.

Rep rows 1–12 for patt.

BACK PANEL

With larger 32"-long needle, CO 44 sts, do not join in the rnd. Purl 1 row.

Beg basket weave patt and work until piece measures 20 (21, 22, 23, 24)".

Place 9 (8, 7, 5, 4) sts on holder for shoulder, place center 26 (28, 30, 34, 36) sts on holder for back neck, place rem 9 (8, 7, 5, 4) sts on holder for shoulder.

FRONT PANEL

Work as for back until piece measures 18 (19, 20, 21, 22)".

Shape neck: Keeping in patt, work 14 (13, 12, 10, 9) sts, place center 16 (18, 20, 24, 26) sts on holder, attach new ball of yarn and work rem 14 (13, 12, 10, 9) sts.

Working each side separately, dec 1 st at each neck edge every row 5 times (either K2tog or P2tog)—9 (8, 7, 5, 4) sts each side.

Cont in patt until piece measures 20 (21, 22, 23, 24)".

Sew shoulders: Mark center 6 (6½, 7, 8, 8½)" for neck opening on front and back panels. With RS facing tog and larger needle, join front and back shoulders tog using 3-needle BO (see page 8).

RIGHT SIDE GUSSET

With RS facing you and beg at bottom of back, PU 83 (87, 91, 95, 99) sts to shoulder, PU 83 (87, 91, 95, 99) sts from shoulder to bottom of front—166 (174, 182, 190, 198) sts. Do not join in the rnd. Work 3 rows in garter st.

Change to St st and work for 4 (5, 6, 7, 8)", ending with completed WS row.

SLEEVES

Bring tips of needles tog so that RS are tog. Join first and last 49 (51, 53, 55, 57) sts using 3-needle BO. Fasten off but do not cut yarn. Turn work to RS. Using smaller 16"-long needle, PU 1 st at seam, work 68 (72, 76, 80, 84) sts, PU 1 st at seam—70 (74, 78, 82, 96) sts. Pm, join in the rnd. Work in St st for 2½".

Dec rnd: K2tog after marker, knit to last 2 sts before marker, K2tog.

Rep dec rnd every 6th row 12 more times—44 (48, 52, 56, 60) sts.

Cont until sleeve measures 15½ (16, 16, 16, 16)".

Cuff: Change to smaller 16"-long needle and work ribbing patt as follows:

> Rnds 1 and 3: Purl.
>
> Rnds 2, 4, 6, 8, 10, 12, 14, and 16: Knit.
>
> Rnds 5, 7, 9, 11, and 13: (K2, P2) around.
>
> Rnds 15 and 17: Purl.

Loosely BO all sts knitwise.

LEFT SIDE GUSSET

Work as for right side gusset except PU sts beg at bottom front to shoulder, then from shoulder to bottom back.

Work second sleeve as first sleeve.

NECKBAND

With RS facing you, smaller 16"-long needle, and beg at left neck edge, PU 68 (76, 84, 92, 100) sts around neck, including sts on holders. Pm, join in the rnd. Work as for sleeve cuff.

BOTTOM BAND

With RS facing you, 32"-long needle, and beg at side seam, PU 160 (176, 192, 208, 224) sts. Pm, join in the rnd. Work as for sleeve cuff.

Weave in ends.

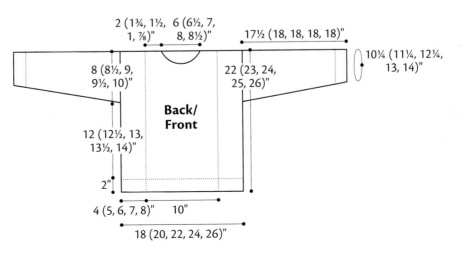

Patti

Who needs a jacket with this easy and quick-to-knit cardigan? This project has only a small seam at the underarm.

Skill Level: Easy ◼◼◻◻

Sizes: S (M, L, XL, 2XL)

Finished Bust: 36 (40, 44, 48, 52)"

Finished Length: 23 (24, 25, 26, 27)"

MATERIALS

7 (8, 9, 10, 11) skeins of Iceland from Crystal Palace Yarns (100% wool; 100 g/3.5 oz]; 100 m/109 yds) in color 452 Field and Stream ⑤

Size 10½ (6.5 mm) circular needles (16" and 32" long)

3 buttons, ¾" diameter

4 stitch holders

2 detachable markers or safety pins

Size I/9 (5.5 mm) crochet hook

Tapestry needle

Gauge: 14 sts and 21 rows = 4" in rev St st

REVERSE STOCKINETTE STITCH

(Worked over any number of sts)

Back and forth:

Row 1 (RS): Purl.

Row 2 (WS): Knit.

Rep rows 1 and 2 for patt.

In the round:

Every rnd: Purl.

BOTTOM

Bottom is worked from side to side.

CO 42 (44, 46, 48, 49) sts. Work in rev St st for 36 (40, 44, 48, 52)", place detachable marker at beg of row when piece measures 9 (10, 11, 12, 13)" from beg, and another detachable marker at 27 (30, 33, 36, 39)" from beg. BO all sts loosely.

RIGHT-FRONT NECK SHAPING

With RS facing you, PU 32 (35, 38, 42, 45) sts along right side of bottom to first marker, turn. Work in rev St st for 4", ending with completed WS row.

Dec row: P2tog, purl to end.

Cont in rev St st, working dec row at beg of every RS row until 21 (23, 25, 28, 30) sts rem.

Cont in rev St st until piece measures 11 (11½, 12, 12½, 13)". Place sts on holder.

BACK

With RS facing you, PU 64 (70, 76, 84, 90) sts along right side of bottom from first marker to 2nd marker, turn. Work in rev St st until piece measures 11 (11½, 12, 12½, 13)", ending with completed RS row. Work 21 (23, 25, 28, 30) sts, BO center 22 (24, 26, 28, 30) sts, work to end. Place sts on holders for shoulders.

LEFT-FRONT NECK SHAPING

With RS facing you, PU 32 (35, 38, 42, 45) sts along right side of bottom from 2nd marker to end. Work in rev St st for 4", ending with completed WS row.

Dec row: Purl to last 2 sts, P2tog.

Cont in rev St st, rep dec row every RS row until 21 (23, 25, 28, 30) sts rem.

Cont in rev St st until piece measures 11 (11½, 12, 12½, 13)", ending with completed WS row. Place sts on holder.

Sew shoulders: Place shoulder sts back on needles. With RS facing tog, join front and back shoulders using 3-needle BO (see page 8).

SLEEVES

Sew side seams 3½" up from bottom piece. With 16"-long needle and beg at armhole, PU 52 (56, 60, 63, 67) sts. Pm, join in the round. Purl every rnd for 3".

Dec rnd: P2tog, purl to last 2 sts before marker, P2tog.

Working in rev St st, rep dec rnd every 5th rnd until 32 (36, 40, 43, 47) sts rem.

Cont in rev St st, work even until sleeve measures 17½ (18, 18, 17½, 17½)". BO all sts loosely. Work 2 rows of sc around wrist. Fasten off.

BAND AND BUTTONHOLES

Beg at bottom left front, work 2 rows of sc around left front, back neck, right front, and bottom. On 2nd rnd, make 3 buttonholes on right front (see photo on page 74) as follows: *ch 2, sk 2 sc, work 2 sc; rep from * 3 times. Fasten off.

Sew buttons opposite buttonholes. Weave in ends.

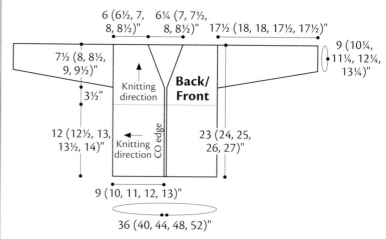

PATTI

STANDARD YARN-WEIGHT SYSTEM

Yarn-Weight Symbol and Category Names	Super Fine ①	Fine ②	Light ③	Medium ④	Bulky ⑤	Super Bulky ⑥
Types of Yarns in Category	Sock, Fingering, Baby	Sport, Baby	DK, Light Worsted	Worsted, Afghan, Aran	Chunky, Craft, Rug	Bulky, Roving
Knit-Gauge Ranges in Stockinette Stitch to 4"	27 to 32 sts	23 to 26 sts	21 to 24 sts	16 to 20 sts	12 to 15 sts	6 to 11 sts
Recommended Needle in U.S. Size Range	1 to 3	3 to 5	5 to 7	7 to 9	9 to 11	11 and larger
Recommended Needle in Metric Size Range	2.25 to 3.25 mm	3.25 to 3.75 mm	3.75 to 4.5 mm	4.5 to 5.5 mm	5.5 to 8 mm	8 mm and larger

SKILL LEVELS

■□□□ **Beginner:** Projects for first-time knitters using basic knit and purl stitches; minimal shaping.

■■□□ **Easy:** Projects using basic stitches, repetitive stitch patterns, and simple color changes; simple shaping and finishing.

■■■□ **Intermediate:** Projects using a variety of stitches, such as basic cables and lace, simple intarsia, and techniques for double-pointed needles and knitting in the round; midlevel shaping.

■■■■ **Experienced:** Projects using advanced techniques and stitches, such as short rows, Fair Isle, more intricate intarsia, cables, lace patterns, and numerous color changes.

METRIC CONVERSIONS

Yards x .91 = meters

Meters x 1.09 = yards

Grams x .035 = ounces

Ounces x 28.35 = grams

Abbreviations

( )	Work instructions within parentheses as directed.	K	knit	rnd(s)	round(s)
*	Repeat instructions following the single asterisk as directed.	K2tog	knit 2 stitches together as 1 (1 stitch decreased)	RS	right side(s)
		LH	left hand	sc	single crochet
approx	approximately	M1	make 1 stitch (1 stitch increased)	sk	skip
beg	begin(ning)			sl	slip
BO	bind off	MC	main color	sl1p	slip 1 stitch purlwise
CC	contrasting color	oz	ounces	ssk	slip 1 stitch as if to knit, slip 1 more stitch as if to knit, return stitches to left needle, and knit them together through back loop (1 stitch decreased)
ch	chain	P	purl		
cn	cable needle	patt	pattern		
CO	cast on	pm	place marker		
cont	continue(ing)	P2tog	purl 2 stitches together as 1 (1 stitch decreased)		
dec	decrease(ing)(s)			st(s)	stitch(es)
dpn(s)	double-pointed needle(s)	PU	pick up and knit	St st	Stockinette stitch
EOR	every other row	rem	remain(ing)	tog	together
g	gram(s)	rep(s)	repeat(s)	wyif	with yarn in front
inc	increase(ing)(s)	rev St st	reverse stockinette stitch	WS	wrong side(s)
		RH	right hand	yds	yards
				YO	yarn over

Suppliers

Contact the following companies to locate shops that carry the yarns featured in this book.

Berroco, Inc.
www.berroco.com
Blackstone Tweed
Bonsai
Ultra Alpaca

Cascade Yarns
www.cascadeyarns.com
Cloud 9
Jewel Hand Dyed
Sierra
Venezia

Crystal Palace Yarns
www.straw.com
Bamboozle
Iceland
Taos

Frog Tree
www.frogtreeyarns.com
Pima Silk

Knitting Fever, Inc.
www.knittingfever.com
King Tut

Kollage Yarns
www.kollageyarns.com
Corntastic

Plymouth Yarn Co.
www.plymouthyarn.com
Fantasy Naturale
Jeannee
Distributes Filatura Cervinia in USA

Universal Yarn
www.universalyarn.com
Deluxe Worsted
Fresco
Sonnet
Distributes Wisdom Yarns in USA

Westminster Fibers, Inc.
www.westminsterfibers.com
Felted Tweed
Distributes Rowan Yarns in USA

About the Author

Andra Knight-Bowman has been designing since she was a small child. She learned so much about designing and writing patterns when she owned a yarn shop for five years.

Andra has written numerous patterns for *Creative Knitting* and Love of Knitting magazines. Previous books are *Easy Cable Knits for all Seasons* (Martingale & Company, 2009), showing the ease of cables; *Modular Knitting Made Easy* (DRG Publishing, 2009), 14 clever designs using the modular technique; and *Fun to Knit Doll Clothes* (DRG Publishing, 2009), eight designs for the popular 18" doll.

She lives in Gray, Tennessee, with her husband and two cats, Billie and Blue.

There's More Online!
- Find more exciting books on knitting, crochet, quilting, and more at www.martingale-pub.com.

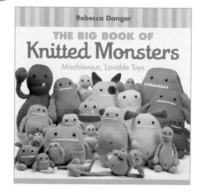
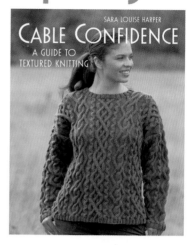

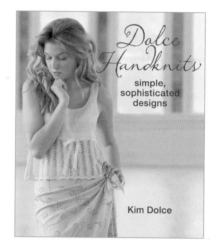

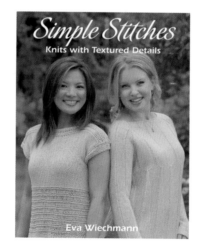
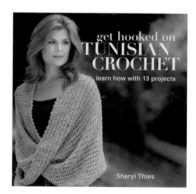